ORGY PLUS MASSACRE

SEXY, SCARY & SENSATIONAL CINEMA 1950-1979

VOLUME 2 (1957-1959)

CREDITS

ORGY + MASSACRE V.2
ISBN 978-1-917285-61-2
Edited by G.H. Janus
Text and images copyright © Black Gas Entertainment 2025
https://black-gas.org
Published by Black Gas Books 2025
In association with The Nocturne Group
All world rights reserved
Design template copyright © Broken Fang Cryptography
Published under licence from Fabbrica Sodoma Productions

CONTENTS

FOREWORD	005
HORROR	007
MAYHEM	055
MYTH	089
SCI-FI	103
SEX	163
INDEX	179

FOREWORD

After working with the Nocturne Group on two anthologies of material selected from their ongoing series of books on early cinema,[1] I was delighted when they offered me the chance to edit a new set of film books using photographs and previously unpublished texts from their post-1949 archive. This mass of material was originally to be developed for inclusion in their original series, but was set aside when it became clear that to produce books equally in-depth for the years 1950 onwards would take decades. Instead, I now have the opportunity to include a selection of these basic but still informative texts to enhance this collection of rare production stills.

As such, the ORGY PLUS MASSACRE series will present a visually-led sampling of sexy, scary and sensational cinema from the years 1950 to 1979, three of the most consequential decades in film history. It was during these years that global cinema came of age, not only in the technological sense but especially by way of pushing back the old restrictions of censorship, so much so that by the end of the 1960s, explicit sex and graphic violence had both become accepted in the mainstream. This new liberalism peaked in the mid-70s, when pretty much anything could be legally seen on commercially available film in one form in another, from picture houses to backstreet projection booths. Of course, this provoked an inevitable backlash in the 1980s, but ORGY PLUS MASSACRE will focus purely on these years when film-makers were free to express their most expansive, excessive and extreme visions on celluloid.

Volume 2 includes more than 150 rare and unusual photographs, with accompanying texts, from the years 1957 to 1959. The book is divided into five sections: Horror, Mayhem (delinquency, crime, murder, atrocity), Myth (fantasies of the near and distant past), Science Fiction, and last but not least, Sex (nudity, sexploitation, pornography[2]). When a film falls into more than one category, as many do, the most dominant theme was chosen.

I now look forward to working on the next volumes of this series, with each one revealing how cinema grew sexier, scarier and more sensational with every passing year.

–G.H. Janus

1. The series from the Nocturne Group is entitled SHADOWS IN A PHANTOM EYE, and documents the years 1872 to 1949. I have edited two anthologies of material taken from the series, SATANIC SHADOWS and BEASTS AND BEAUTIES. These represent just a fraction of the content that the series, which runs to 15 volumes and well over 3,000 pages, has to offer.

2. Yes, even in the 1950s and 1960s loops of pornographic film were available, screened in the most clandestine venues or sold under counters, a situation which continued until Denmark led the legalization of such material from 1968-69 onwards.

I WAS A TEENAGE WEREWOLF
Production: USA, 1957
Director: Gene Fowler Jr
Category: Horror/Science Fiction

HORROR

BACK FROM THE DEAD
Production: USA, 1957
Director: Charles Marquis Warren
Category: Horror
Obscure, low-budget Satanist flick in which a man loses his wife to a dangerous cult of devil-worshippers; when he remarries, his pious new bride becomes possessed by his first wife's demonic spirit. The curse is finally lifted when Father Renall, the cult leader, is murdered by a jealous member of his coven.

BLOOD OF DRACULA
Production: USA, 1957
Director: Herbert L. Strock
UK release title: **Blood Is My Heritage**
Category: Horror
No Dracula, but a teenage girl who turns into a vampire under hypnosis in this she-power companion to Strock's **I Was A Teenage Frankenstein** and Gene Fowler's **I Was A Teenage Werewolf**, featuring a barely disguised lesbian villainess and a hideous rock and roll interlude. Strock also directed **How To Make A Monster** (1958), with double vampire/werewolf horrors.

CAT GIRL
Production: UK, 1957
Director: Alfred Shaughnessy
Category: Horror
A British take on Val Lewton's **Cat People**, with Barbara Shelley as the girl with a feline curse. The main difference is that her apparent transformations are spurred by anger, as opposed to the sexual arousal implied by Lewton.

THE CURSE OF FRANKENSTEIN
Production: UK, 1957
Director: Terence Fisher
Category: Horror/Science Fiction
The decision by Hammer Films, an independent British production company, to make its own update of Mary Shelley's *Frankenstein* in 1957 was a landmark one for horror cinema. Scriptwriter Jimmy Sangster based his screenplay on the original book, rather than Universal's classic horror film of 1931, but the plot nevertheless turned out much the same, with the Baron Victor Frankenstein (played by Peter Cushing) allowing his scientific zeal to get the better of him when he murders a great scientist in order to obtain his brain to put into the creature he is covertly

assembling from human parts. His associate, Paul Krempe, is so horrified that he tries to stop Frankenstein; in their struggle the brain is damaged so that when the creature comes to life it possesses violent criminal tendencies, which result in a series of murders for which Frankenstein is blamed and condemned to death at the guillotine. For the creature's appearance, Hammer came up with something resembling an animated human corpse, while Peter Cushing's characterisation of the Baron was also remarkable, presenting him as an arrogant, cruel, rebellious figure; so strong was his portrayal that it was he, rather than the creature, who would return in the subsequent films, each time bringing to life some new monstrosity. Hammer's vibrant use of colour – uncommon at the time, and not previously seen in British horror – was highly effective in heightening the impact of bleeding parts and fiery violence; the creature's face being blasted away by a shotgun was a particularly gruesome scene of bloody mayhem. Despite a critical savaging – it was roundly condemned as being shocking, sick and sadistic – **Curse Of Frankenstein** turned out to be a big success in England, and also the biggest dollar-earner that any British studio produced that year; the age of Hammer Horror had arrived.

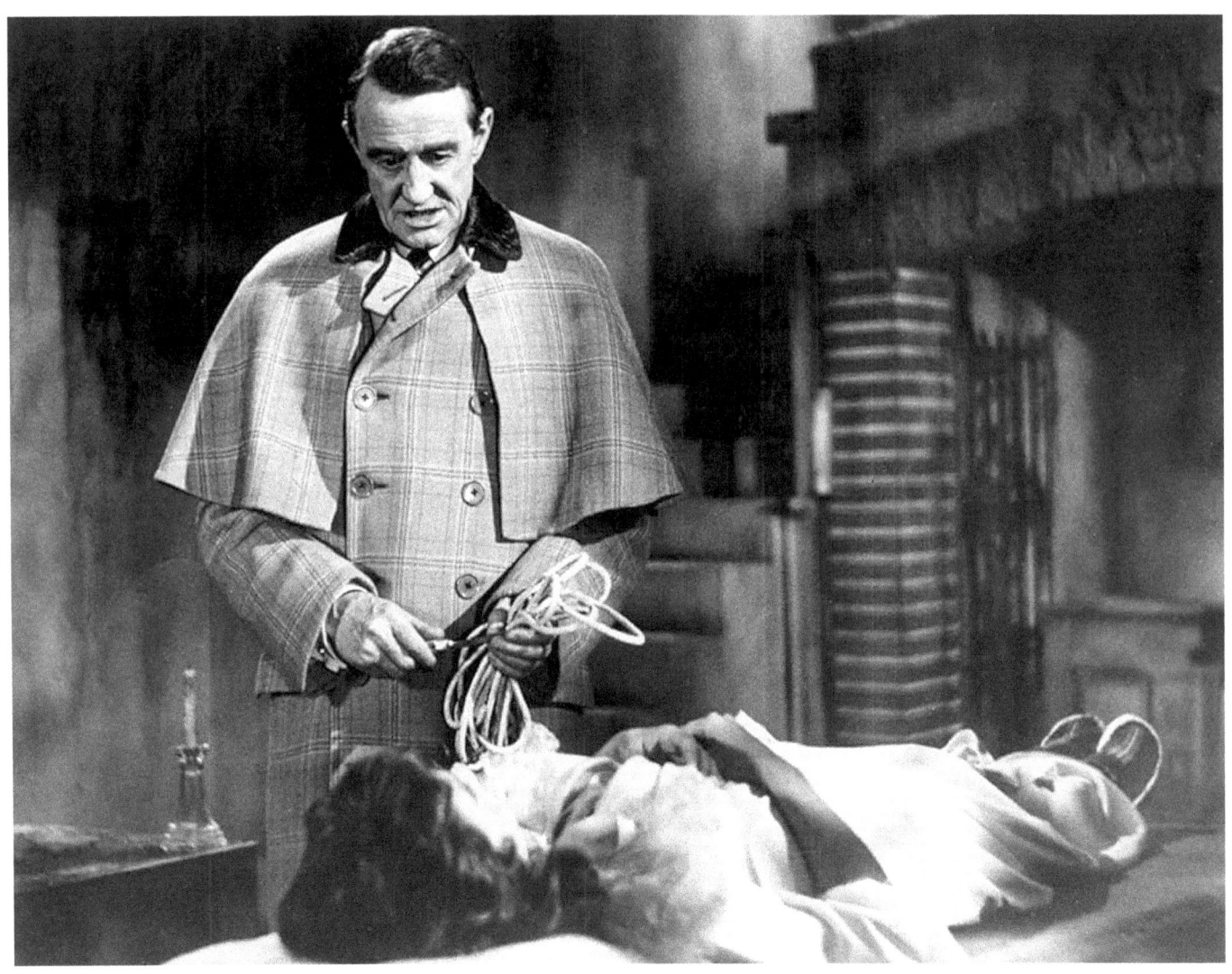

DAUGHTER OF DR. JEKYLL

Production: USA, 1957
Director: Edgar G. Ulmer
Category: Horror/Science Fiction

Late attempt by Ulmer to recreate the mood of the classic Universal horror movies of the 1930s, adding elements of lycanthropy and vampirism to a metamorphic mystery. Vivid dream sequences and expressionistic lighting, fog machines and miniature sets all contribute to one of the director's better short features (clocking in at 70 minutes) from the final stages of his career.

THE GLASS EYE

Production: USA, 1957
Director: Robert Stevens
Category: Horror

Perhaps the most outstanding – and unsettling – episode from the entire television series **Alfred Hitchcock Presents**, which ran from 1955 to 1962, the best years of Hitchcock's career (during this period he directed **Vertigo**, his swirling tale of obsession and madness, plus the horror classics **Psycho** and **The Birds**). **The Glass Eye** was scripted by Sterling Silliphant, and featuring both William Shatner and malignant dwarf Billy Barty (as a ventriloquist's dummy).

I BURY THE LIVING
Production: USA, 1957
Director: Albert Band
Category: Horror
Set in a Los Angeles graveyard, this B-horror movie starts with the discovery by the cemetery manager that he has the power over life and death by using pins and a map of his burial plots. The film's haunted mood is sustained by the lighting and design, but is broken by a rather lame dénouement that spoils an intriguing premise.

I WAS A TEENAGE FRANKENSTEIN
Production: USA, 1957
Director: Herbert L. Strock
Category: Horror/Science Fiction

KAIDAN KASANE-GA-FUCHI
("Ghost Story Of Kasane Swamp")
Production: Japan, 1957
Director: Nobuo Nakagawa
Category: Horror

One of many film adaptations of the classic horror tale *Shinkei Kasane-ga-fuchi* by Encho Sanyuutei I, written around 1860. Nakagawa was one of Japan's leading horror film directors, and his version of the story, in which a *samurai* is haunted by the disfigured ghost of a blind masseur he killed and buried in a swamp, remains notable for its elements of stylized grotesquerie, death and retribution. Nakagawa's masterpiece was **Jigoku** ("Hell", 1960), with its brutal, bloody and surrealistic torture visions of the Buddhist inferno. The blind masseur became a staple motif in Japanese horror, featuring in other movies such as Kazuo Mori's **Kaidan kokuidori** ("Ghost Story Of Kakui Street", 1961), Kazuo Hase's **Kaidan zankoku monogatari**, ("Cruel Ghost Story", 1968 – actually based on a novelisation of the original *Kasane* story), and Yasuzo Masumura's **Moju** ("Blind Beast", 1969).

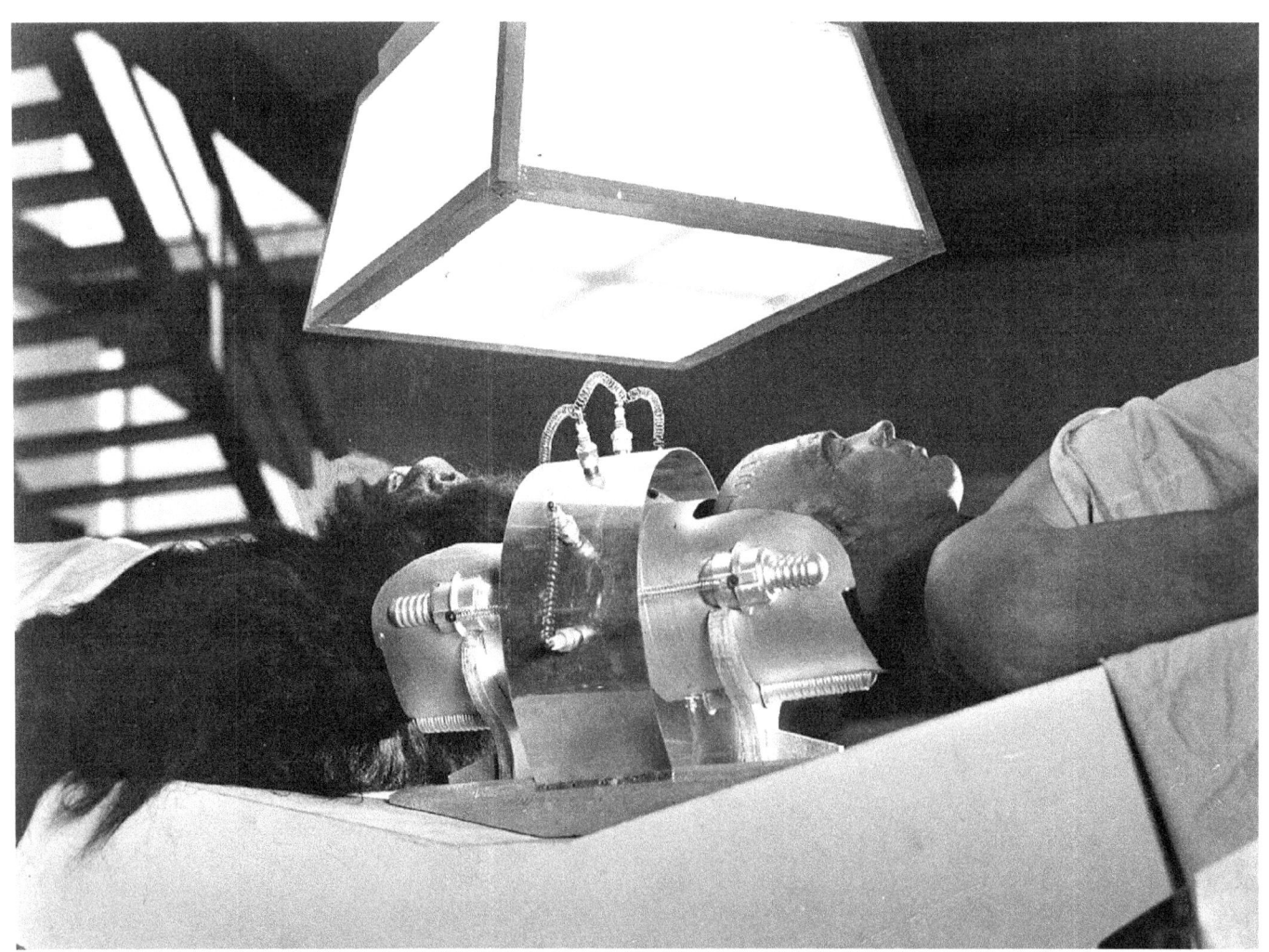

LADRÓN DE CADÁVERES
("The Corpse-Stealer")
Production: Mexico, 1957
Director: Fernando Méndez
Category: Horror/Science Fiction

LA MOMIA AZTECA
("The Aztec Mummy")
Production: Mexico, 1957
Director: Rafael Lopez Portillo
Category: Horror

Transposing the traditional Egyptian mummy horror story to Mexico, director Portillo came up with Popoca, a long-haired Aztec corpse that kills. Portillo directed two sequels: **La Maldición De La Momia Azteca** ("Curse Of The Aztec Mummy", 1957) and **La Momia Azteca Contra El Robot Humano** ("The Aztec Mummy Versus The Human Robot", 1958). The latter film was described as featuring a "relentless machine battling a gruesome corpse", and is notable for Aztec dance sequences choreographed by actress Stella Inda. René Cardona's **Las Luchadoras Contra La Momia** (She-Wrestlers Versus The Mummy", 1964) featured a different mummy (named Xochitl).

NIGHT OF THE DEMON
Production: UK, 1957
Director: Jacques Tourneur
US release title: **Curse Of The Demon**
Category: Horror/Satanism
One of several films to feature a magus-type character said to have been inspired by the English occultist Aleister Crowley, here named Dr. Julian Karlswell; he ends up being destroyed by the very demon he summons to kill others. The story is loosely based on M.R. James' supernatural story "Casting The Runes" (1911).

SPOOK CHASERS
Production: USA, 1957
Director: George Blair
Category: Horror-Comedy

TEENAGE MONSTER
Production: USA, 1957
Director: Jacques R. Marquette
Category: Horror/Western

THE VAMPIRE
Production: USA, 1957
Director: Paul Landres
Category: Science Fiction/Horror
As in **The Werewolf** from the previous year, the monster in **The Vampire** is created by an accident of science – in this case, by ingesting an experimental drug made from bat's blood.

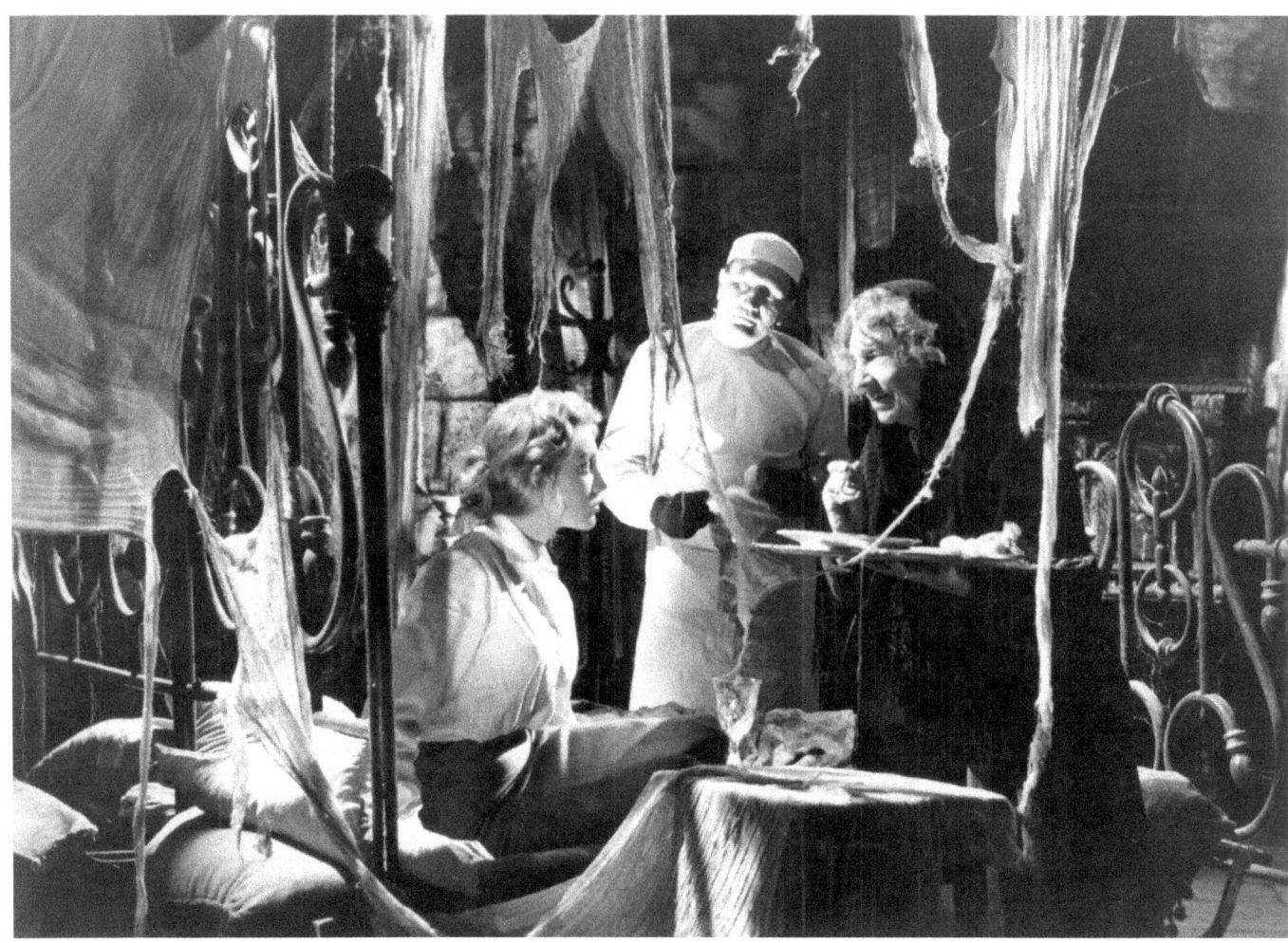

I VAMPIRI
("The Vampires")
Production: Italy, 1957
Director: Riccardo Freda
Category: Horror
Italian gothic, photographed (and some say completed) by Mario Bava, a variation on the Erzsebey Bathory legend set in Paris, where a deranged old duchess and a crazy scientist team up to drain blood from local girls. Known in the USA as **Lust Of The Vampire**, and regarded as the first Italian horror film of the post-war period.

EL VAMPIRO
("The Vampire")
Production: Mexico, 1957
Director: Fernando Méndez
Category: Horror

The best Mexican vampire movie, thankfully largely devoid of the silliness, wrestlers and unwelcome humour that ruins so many of Mexico's otherwise effective horror efforts. Shot in monochrome with gothic sets and lighting, with a mesmeric performance by Germán Robles as the vampire, Count Karol de Lavud. Both director and star were back for the sequel, **El Ataúd Del Vampiro**, a year later.

VOODOO ISLAND
Production: USA, 1957
Director: Reginald Le Borg
Category: Horror

YOJASO NO MAOU
("Demon King Of Snake Mansion")
Production: Japan, 1957
Director: Morihei Magatani
Category: Horror/Science Fiction

The Japanese horror film genre only began to blossom in the 1950s, and **Yojaso No Maou** is an outstanding example of the grotesque style which would mark the best of those emerging movies. A variation on *Island Of Lost Souls*, this gothic freak-film concerns a crazed surgeon who creates man-beast hybrids, assisted by a twisted hunchback. Produced by Shintoho, whose *ero-gro* flavoured horror output also included such items as **Kenpei to barabara shibijin** ("Secret Police: Dismembered Beauty", 1957) and **Kyujukyu-honme no kimusume** ("The 99th Virgin", 1959).

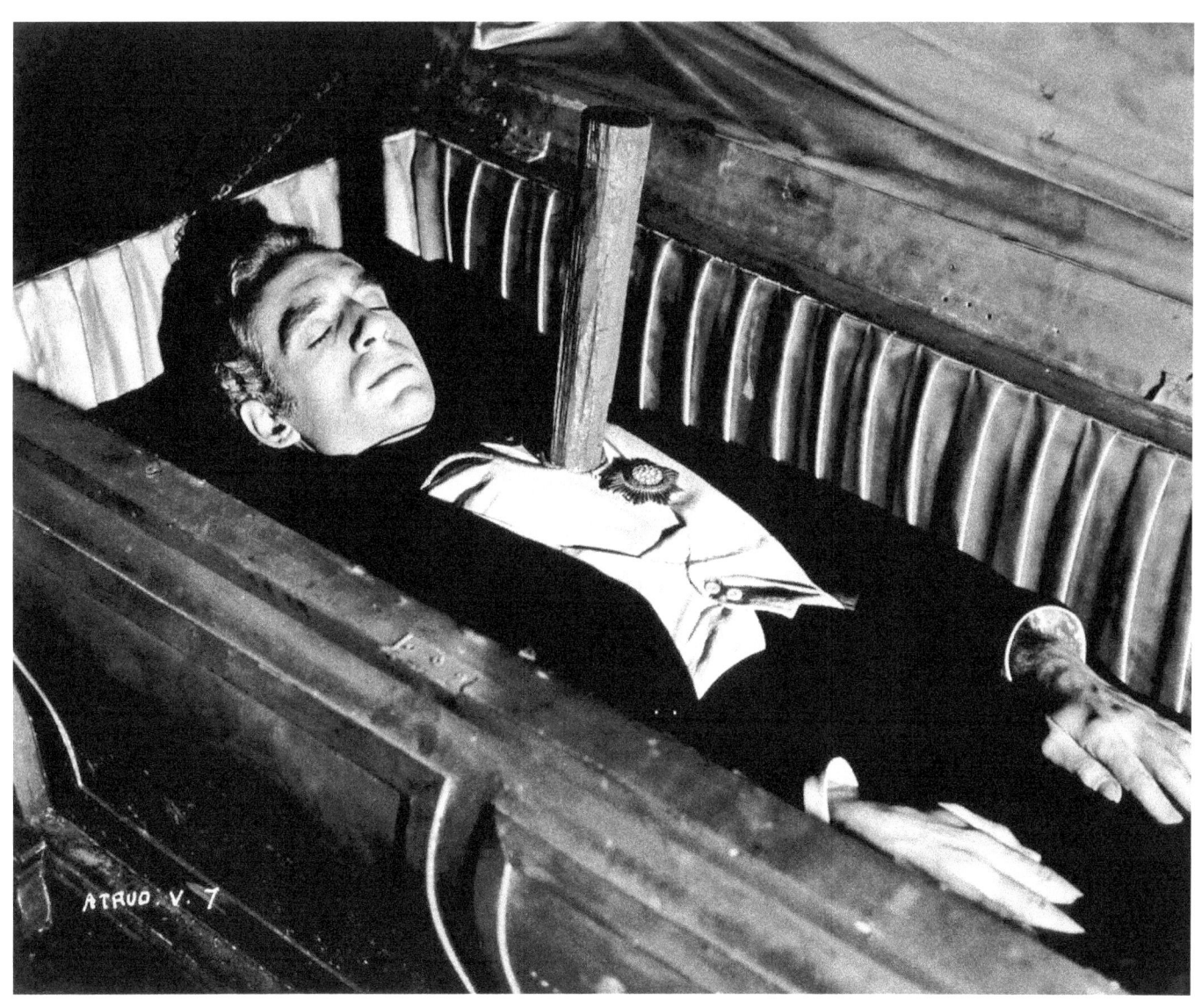

EL ATAÚD DEL VAMPIRO
("The Vampire's Coffin")
Production: Mexico, 1958
Director: Fernando Méndez
Category: Horror

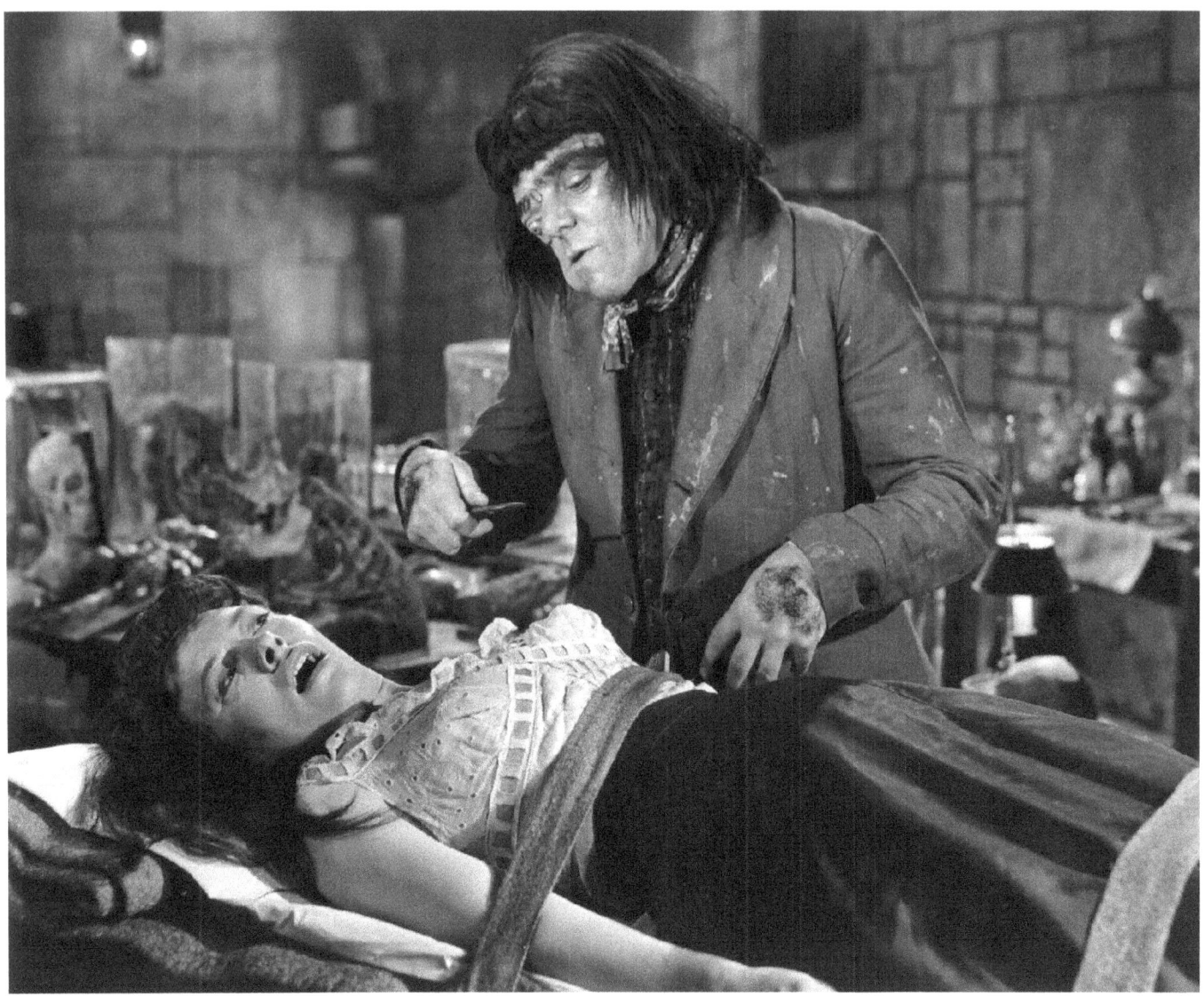

BLOOD OF THE VAMPIRE
Production: UK, 1958
Director: Henry Cass
Category: Horror
Like Freda's **I Vampiri,** this is not really a vampire movie, as the fiend in question is in fact a deranged scientist who drains his young female victims of blood in order to carry out medical experiments. His assistant is a hideously deformed hunchback. Really notable only for its sadistic elements, conjured up by the images of women chained, tortured and exsanguinated in subterranean dungeons.

BYAKUYA NO YOJO
("Sorceress Of The White Night")
Production: Japan, 1958
Director: Eisuke Takizawa
Category: Black Magic
This Nikkatsu horror-fantasy film tells of a wandering monk who encounters a seductive witch and her drooling, imbecilic dwarf husband, played by Tadashi Kobayashi. The witch fornicates with every man she lures and then turns them into beasts, but the monk's purity threatens to disrupt her rampage of sex and evil.

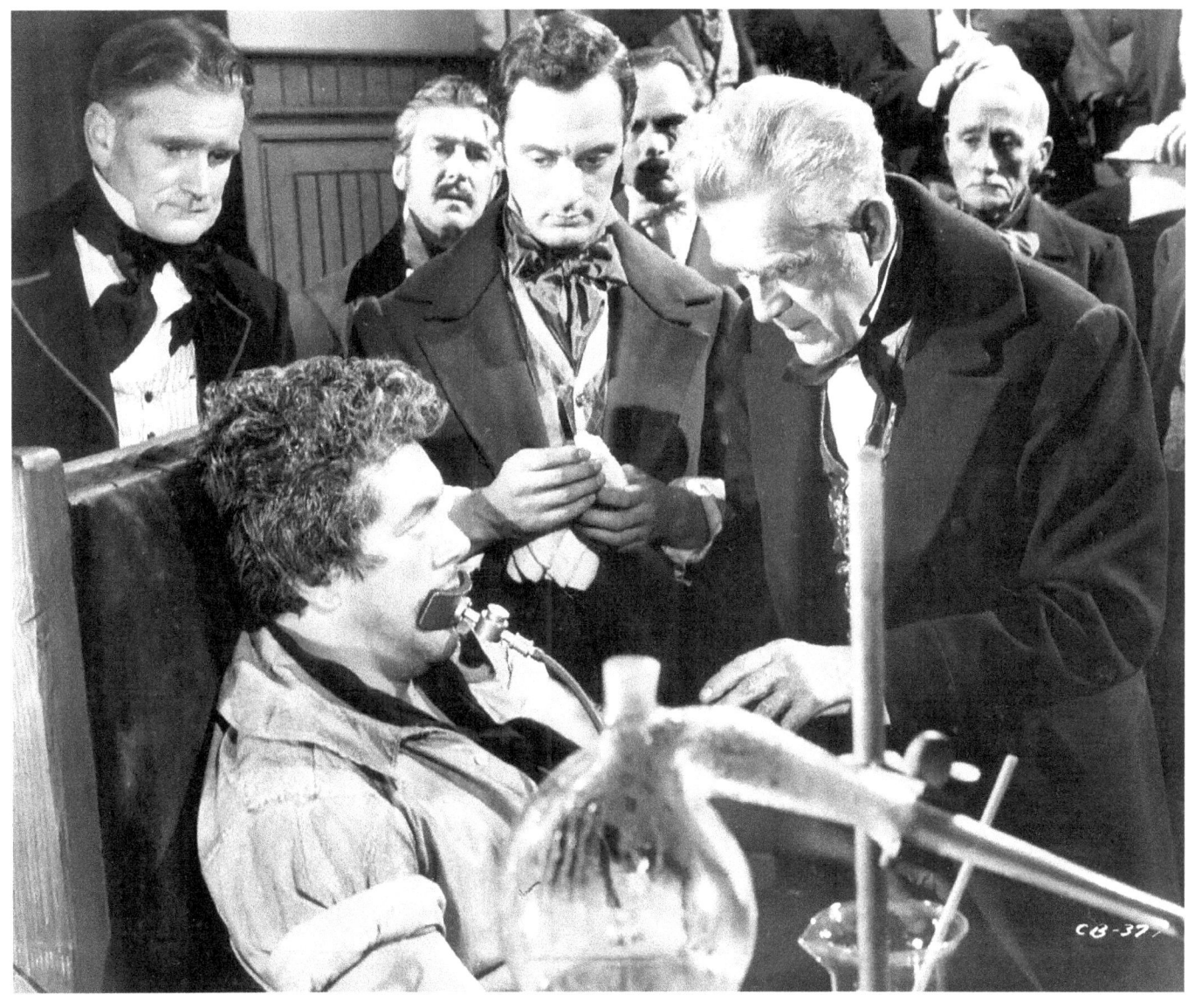

CORRIDORS OF BLOOD
Production: UK, 1958
Director: Robert Day
Category: Horror

With its basic storyline of surgeons operating on various patients without anaesthetic, **Corridors Of Blood** seems little more than an excuse to depict successive acts of mutilation – what a brilliant concept. Christopher Lee appears as Resurrection Joe, a gaunt grave-robber who supplies a drug-addicted doctor (Boris Karloff) with cadavers. Set in Victorian times, the film has its minor place in both the "medical horror" and "drug abuse" sub-genres.

THE DEVIL'S PARTNER
Production: USA, 1958
Director: Charles R. Rondeau
Category: Horror
Not released until 1961, **The Devil's Partner** is a black magic movie set in the small Texas town of Furnace Flats, where a mysterious stranger arrives to attend the funeral of his uncle, who was regarded locally as a Devil-worshipper. Soon the stranger (named Nick) is seen killing goats and drawing talismans on his floor, and the local animals go crazy, in some cases killing their owners. Eventually the truth is uncovered when the sheriff shoots a snake which transforms itself first into Nick and then into his uncle; all were aspects of the same Satanic creature, which is finally exorcised by a priest. One of the first examples of witchcraft in a rural, rather than urban, setting, and pre-dating the likes of Jack Starrett's **Race With The Devil**.

DE DØDES TJERN
("Lake Of The Dead")
Production: Norway, 1958
Director: Kåre Bergstrøm
Category: Horror
The first feature-length Norwegian horror film, renowned for its fearful aura and crystalline black-and-white cinematography.

DRACULA
Production: UK, 1958
Director: Terence Fisher
US release title: **Horror Of Dracula**
Category: Horror

After the great success of **The Curse Of Frankenstein** in 1957, Hammer Films were quick to follow up with this technicolor update of the original 1930 **Dracula**. Starring Christopher Lee as the vampire Count, it proved to be another landmark production. Lee's portrayal quickly became regarded as so definitive that whenever people thought of Dracula, they envisioned Lee. His image, darkly virile and sexually-charged, lips glossed with bright blood, virtually revolutionised the global horror movie industry. Peter Cushing played the Count's perennial nemesis, the eminent vampirologist Dr. Van Helsing. Filmed in opulent colours, the film was far more explicit than the earlier Lugosi version both in sexuality and bloodshed, with Dracula's female victims clearly enjoying rather than resisting his neck-biting advances. Van Helsing's comparison of vampirism to drug addiction underlines the theme of disease and delirium exemplified by director Fisher's "sadism" and "sexual disgust" in the shots where Lucy's unclean flesh is seared by a crucifix, while the inexorable invasion of both Mina's pristine home and her body by the vampire, while her protectors stand impotently in the grounds, illustrates perfectly his concept of the "beast within", the devil virus in the virgin flesh.

THE FACE IN THE TOMBSTONE MIRROR
Production: USA, 1958
Director: Curt Siodmak
Category: Horror/Science Fiction
In late 1957, Hammer Films chief executive Michael Carreras flew to Hollywood to supervise production on a new Columbia TV series, to be entitled **Tales Of Frankenstein** and to be based on the style of Hammer's first two **Frankenstein** films.

It appears however that Columbia in fact were only interested in appropriating the Hammer name to promote a lacklustre and largely unrelated series. A 30-minute pilot, **The Face In The Tombstone Mirror**, directed by horror veteran Siodmak and starring Anton Diffring as the Baron and Don Megowen as an oriental-looking monster, was filmed but rarely screened.

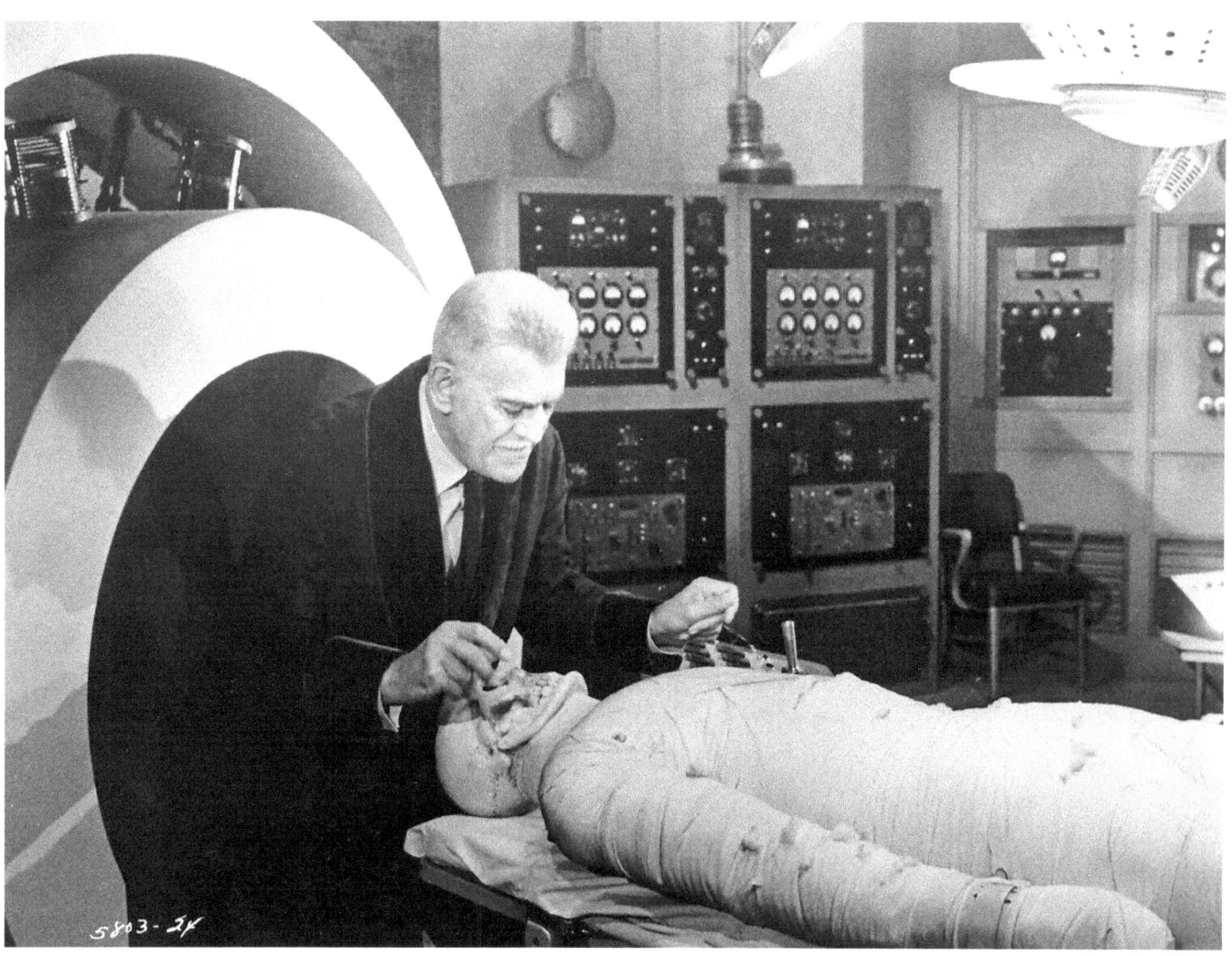

FRANKENSTEIN 1970
Production: USA, 1958
Director: Howard W. Koch
Category: Horror/Science Fiction

Boris Karloff's first appearance in a Frankenstein film since 1939, but here he plays the elderly Baron who, having been badly tortured by Nazis, has a horribly scarred face and is forced to rent out his castle to film-crews as a movie set. It also seems that the Baron – on the hunt for eyeballs – has been making monsters again, and one lurks in the hidden laboratory beneath the cellars. When this creature – only seen swathed in bandages – starts picking off members of the crew, the local police investigate. The monster finally dies in the lab, and is revealed to have the face, youthful and no longer disfigured, of its creator. Incredibly low-budget, badly edited and strange, **Frankenstein 1970** fails on all normal levels but somehow retains a vestigial power to engage the viewer, if only as a curio of its time.

FRANKENSTEIN'S DAUGHTER
Production: USA, 1958
Director: Richard E. Cunha
Category: Horror/Science Fiction

GRIP OF THE STRANGLER
Production: UK, 1958
Director: Robert Day
US release title: **The Haunted Strangler**
Category: Horror
Shot back-to-back with Day's **Corridors Of Blood**, both films starring Boris Karloff who here plays a novelist who blacks out and commits murders without remembering afterwards, having been possesssed by the spirit of an executed killer through contact with a possessed scalpel.

HOW TO MAKE A MONSTER
Production: USA, 1958
Director: Herbert L. Strock
Category: Horror

MACABRE
Production: USA, 1958
Director: William Castle
Category: Suspense/Horror

Not particularly macabre in its execution, **Macabre** is basically a suspense mystery with some horrific touches, in which a man is given five hours to find his kidnapped daughter, who has been buried alive. What makes it notable is its status as the first in a line of increasingly sensationalistic shock-horror films directed by Castle between 1958 and the mid-60s. For most of these films, Castle came up with an ingenious marketing gimmick, and **Macabre** was no exception – each audience member was issued with a certificate of insurance allegedly worth $1,000 if he or she died of fright during the film. No-one did, but the gimmick worked and set Castle on his way to notoriety and filthy lucre as a kind of "pulp Hitchcock" for the masses.

MISTERIOS DE LA MAGIA NERA
("Mysteries Of Black Magic")
Production: Mexico, 1958
Director: Miguel M. Delgado
Category: Horror

Another vortical black magic tale from the golden age of Mexican horror, in which a 400-year-old sorceress inhabits the young form of a stage magic starlet while her overlord, the "master of the black sabbath", is kept half-alive in his tomb. She is aided by a dwarfish, deformed assistant, and combated by the professor whose future son-in-law she lusts after. With some striking black magic sequences amongst the usual pulp parabolas.

RETURN OF DRACULA
Production: USA, 1958
Director: Paul Landres
Category: Horror

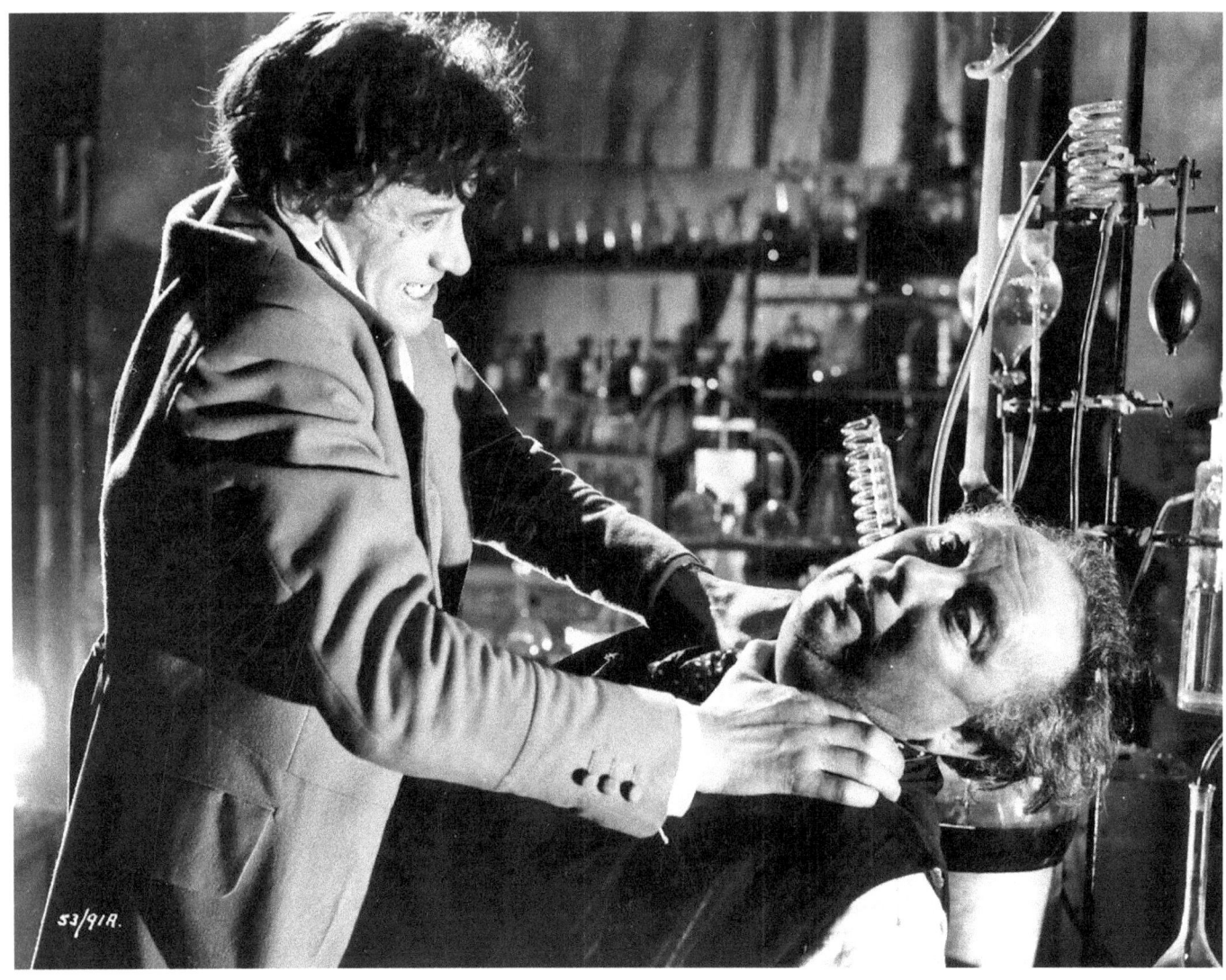

THE REVENGE OF FRANKENSTEIN
Production: UK, 1958
Director: Terence Fisher
Category: Horror/Science Fiction

A quick sequel to Hammer's successful **Curse Of Frankenstein**, **The Revenge Of Frankenstein** saved Peter Cushing's neck from the guillotine poised to sever it at the end of the previous film – a handy priest had taken his place at the beheading – and allowed the Baron to masquerade as a Dr. Stein, continuing his experiments at a poor hospital where he tries to help his deformed assistant Hans (Michael Gwynn) by transplanting his brain to a healthy body. When the brain is damaged in a struggle, Hans turns into a crazed "monster" with an appetite for human flesh. Dr. Stein barely escapes an enraged mob, and eventually takes up residence on London's Harley Street as one Professor Frank. The Baron is here shown is contrasting lights – on the one hand as a dedicated physician struggling to help his patients, on the other as the ruthless experimenter, building composite anatomies from the excised body parts of the inmates themselves. Terence Fisher again directed, carefully elaborating this central dichotomy which is so typical of his protagonists.

THE SCREAMING SKULL
Production: USA, 1958
Director: Alex Nichol
Category: Horror

THE THING THAT COULDN'T DIE
Production: USA, 1958
Director: Will Cowan
Category: Horror
Another film belonging to that rarefied sub-genre, the living severed head movie. A young girl with psychic powers unearths the head of a Spanish Satanist, personally decapitated by Sir Francis Drake in 1579 when he was discovered as a spy amongst Drake's crew. The head comes back to life and begins to exert its evil, Devil-powered will, provoking some unnerving scenes of the Freudian uncanny.

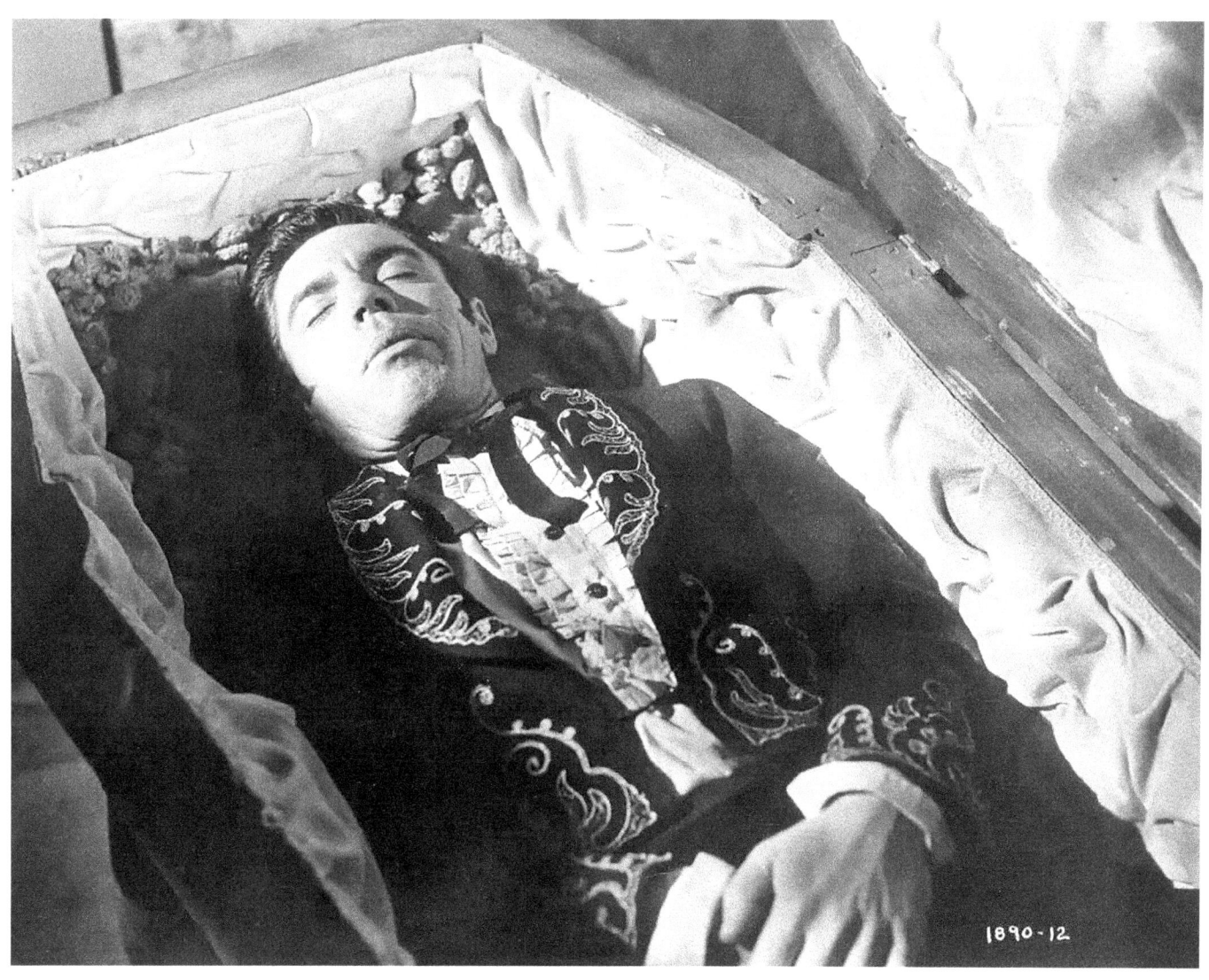

CURSE OF THE UNDEAD
Production: USA, 1959
Director: Edward Dein
Category: Horror
One of the very few films in the sub-sub-genre of the period "vampire western" (the only other one that easily springs to mind is the campy **Billy The Kid Vs Dracula**, with John Carradine). A black-clad hired gun turns out to be one of the undead, and the people of a small California town must finds ways to destroy him.

THE DEVIL'S HAND
Production: USA, 1959/61
Director: William Hole Jr.
Alernative title: **The Naked Goddess**
Category: Horror

A man gets drawn into a devil-worshipping cult who use vooddoo dolls to attract their victims. An intriguing premise, complete with an evil cult master and a sexy witch who lures men to the very gates of Hell, human sacrifices, and an appearance by Bruno VeSota. Produced in 1959 but not released until 1961, this was a one-off excursion into horror for director Hole, although around the same time he also shot some extra footage for the US release of **La Cara Del Terror**, a weird Spanish film based around themes of mental illness and disfigurement.

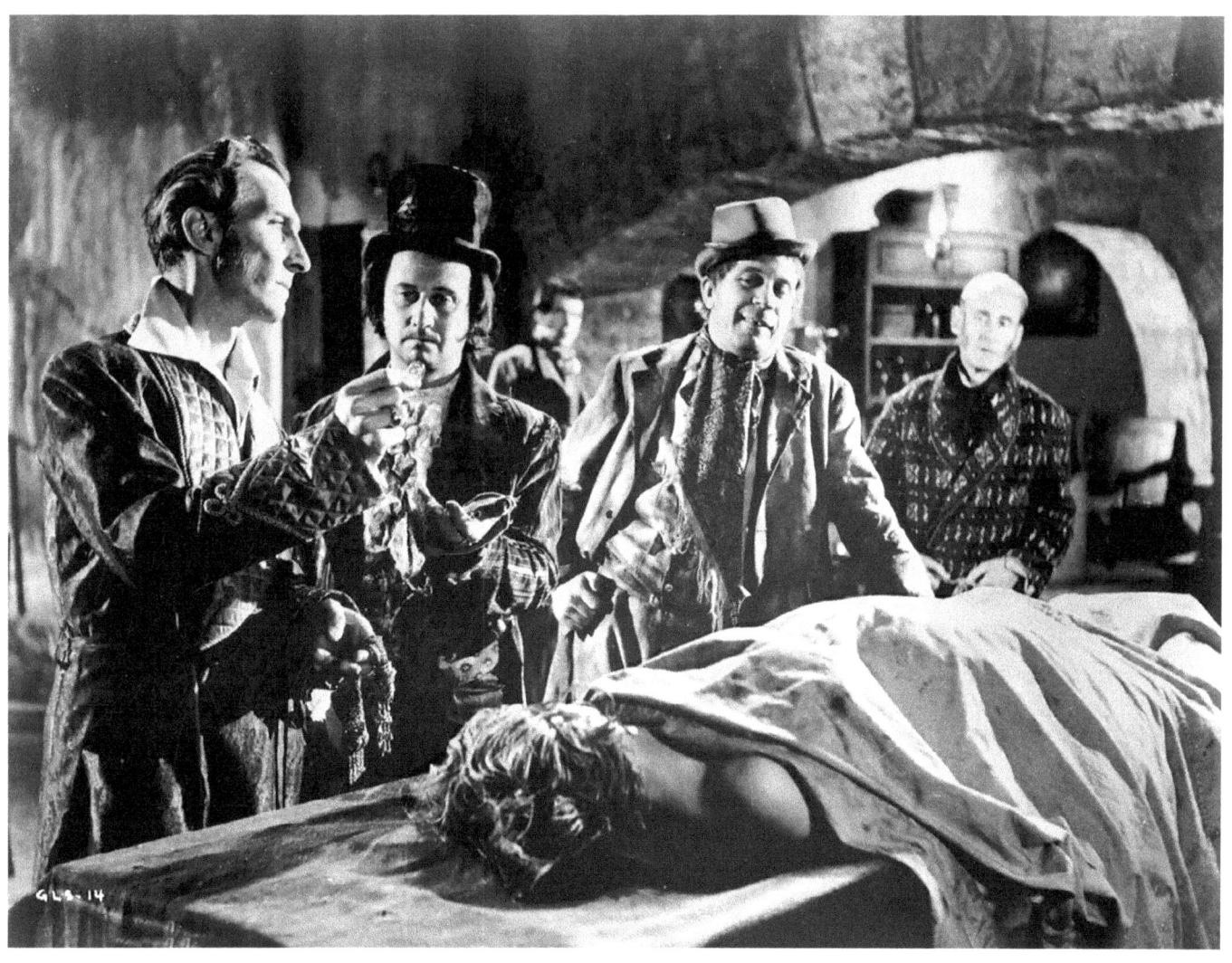

THE FLESH AND THE FIENDS
Production: UK, 1959
Director: John Gilling
Category: Horror
A remake of the Tod Slaughter film **Greed Of William Hart**, concerning those notorious Scottish grave-robbers (actually murderers – they just killed their victims and never stole corpses) Burke and Hare. A good cast, including Peter Cushing, Donald Pleasance and Billie Whitelaw, and some flourishes of gore and violence, make this one of the more effective Baker and Berman productions. A similar story was told two years later in **The Anatomist** (Dennis Vance, 1961), a dreary, verbose story of grave-robbers and the doctor who employs them to dig up cadvers for his classes, then again in the bawdy **Burke And Hare** (1971), and again in the insipid **Doctor And The Devils** (1985), from a script first written by Welsh poet Dylan Thomas in 1965 and suppressed by the censor.

THE FOUR SKULLS OF JONATHAN DRAKE
Production: USA, 1959
Director: Edward L. Cahn
Category: Horror

EL GRITO DE LA MUERTE
("The Scream Of Death")
Production: Mexico, 1959
Director: Fernando Méndez
Category: Horror
A horror-western from Mexico, where weird hybrid genres (a popular one is horror-wrestling) are the norm. A ranching family is haunted by a crying ghost whose children drowned in nearby Skeleton Swamp. Director Méndez made another horror-western, **Los Diablos Del Terror** ("Devils Of Terror") that same year. Another crazed horror-western fusion film from Mexico was **Los Encapuchados Del Infierno** ('The Hooded Ones From Hell", 1962).

EL HOMBRE Y El MONSTRUO
("Man And Monster")
Production: Mexico, 1959
Director: Rafael Baledón
Category: Horror

A variation of the Jekyll and Hyde story. In this version, a mild-mannered man is transformed into a slavering beast not by a potion, but whenever he hears a certain passage of classical music.

THE HOUSE ON HAUNTED HILL
Production: USA, 1959
Director: William Castle
Category: Horror

THE MAN WHO COULD CHEAT DEATH
Production: UK, 1959
Director: Terence Fisher
Category: Horror

The Man Who Could Cheat Death was Hammer's version of **The Man In Half Moon Street,** first filmed by Paramount in 1945. This new treatment starred Anton Diffring as the 104-year-old who keeps himself looking only a third of his age by a periodic gland operation. When his regular surgeon declines to renew the process, he kills him and kidnaps a woman (Hazel Court), blackmailing her surgeon lover (Christopher Lee) into operating on him. He is eventually double-crossed, and lapses hideously into his real age like Oscar Wilde's Dorian Gray, perishing in a dramatically contrived fire.

MISTERIOS DE ULTRATOMBA
("Mysteries Beyond The Grave")
Production: Mexico, 1959
Director: Fernando Méndez
US release title: **The Black Pit Of Dr. M**
Category: Horror

A key Mexican horror film, dealing with death and resurrection, disfigurement, psychopathic violence, murder, ghosts, and the price of peering beyond the tomb.

THE MUMMY

Production: UK, 1959
Director: Terence Fisher
Category: Horror

After the unqualified success of Hammer's **Curse Of Frankenstein** and **Dracula**, the big Hollywood studios were only too happy to admit that the British company had the knack for turning out polished, commercial but economically-budgeted horror pictures, and began to hand over properties they owned for the re-make treatment. For Universal, Jimmy Sangster oversaw **The Mummy**, again bringing together the proven team of Christopher Lee and Peter Cushing. Lee took the title role, his Mummy being that of Kharis, the former lover of an entombed princess who comes to life to avenge the desecration of her tomb by a group of explorers. Only a likeness of a modern woman (Yvonne Furneaux) to his love of old distracts him from his homicidal mission, and he carries her off through a swamp, there to be finally gunned down by a group of pursuers. Cushing plays the woman's husband. Lee makes a very powerful, fast-moving Mummy, and director Terence Fisher shows us Kharis' burial rites with typically sadistic detail: before being interred alive, his tongue is stretched out with pliers and then hacked off with a knife.

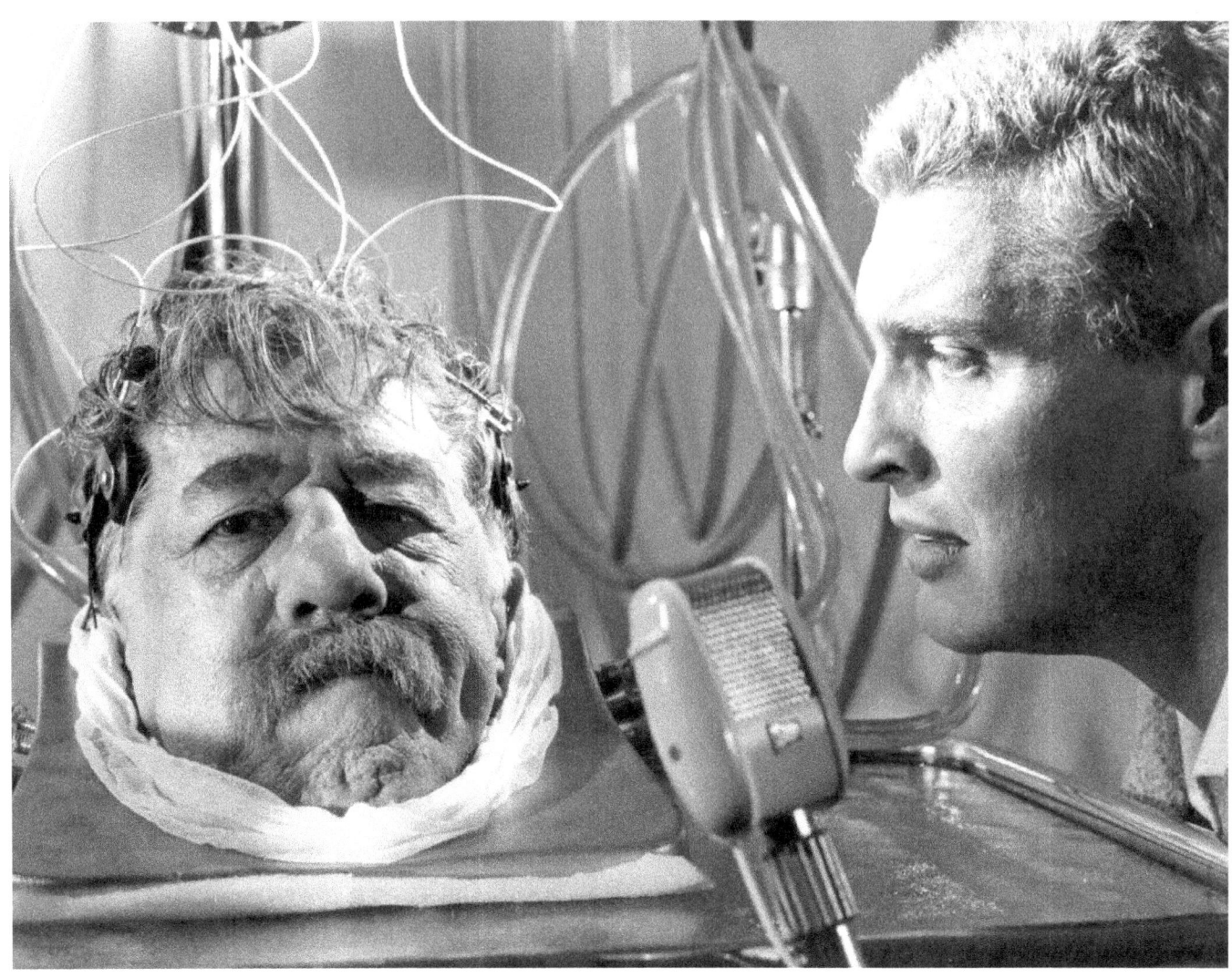

DIE NACKTE UND DER SATAN
("The Nude Girl And The Devil")
Production: Germany, 1959
Director: Victor Trivas
US release title: **The Head**
Category: Horror/Science Fiction
With a slightly misleading original title, this is actually a film about a mad scientist who likes to decapitate people and experiment with the severed heads – sometimes grafting them onto sexy new bodies, sometimes just keeping them alive in a horrifying, disembodied state. A truly bizarre and often disturbing horror movie, filled with mutilations and physical grotesqueries, and set in a hellish, expressionistic milieu of menacing shadows and twisted architecture.

ONNA KYUKETSUKI
("Lady Blood-Sucker")
Production: Japan, 1959
Director: Nobuo Nakawgawa
Category: Horror
Prolific horror director Nakagawa delivers the first Japanese vampire film to feature a proper predatory bloodsucker in the leading role. A Shintoho production, based on a novel by Soto Tachibana.

TERROR IS A MAN
Production: Philippines, 1959
Director: Gerardo de Leon
Category: Horror
Generally regarded as the first Filipino horror movie, this is a take on H.G. Wells' *The Island Of Dr Moreau*, but with one man-beast rather than the many. A dark film with ample gore and sadism for its production year, and a William Castle-like gimmick: a warning bell rings just before the gruesome surgical scenes of flesh being sliced apart. Director de Leon went on to make another Filipino horror classic, **The Blood Drinkers,** before the exotic mutation movies **Brides Of Blood** (1965) and **Mad Doctor Of Blood Island** (1968).

THE TINGLER
Production: USA, 1959
Director: William Castle
Category: Horror
William Castle's outrageous pulp horror trip is still credited as the first film to feature LSD. Vincent Price, in one of his classic roles, plays a scientist who injects himself with acid in order to stimulate the fear response. He has discovered that extreme terror causes the growth of a centipede-like creature in the spinal cord, and selects a deaf/mute woman to literally scare to death. The film features several

typical Castle set-pieces, including taps that run with blood (for which the film briefly turns to colour), while Price's acid-inspired contortions are among the seminal images of drug cinema.

TOKAIDO YOTSUYA KAIDAN
("Tokaido Yotsuya Ghost Story")
Production: Japan, 1959
Director: Nobuo Nakagawa
Category: Horror

One of the best film adaptations of *Tokaido yotsuya kaidan* (1825) by the classical *kabuki* playwright Namboku Tsuruya IV, in which the hideous disfigured ghost of Oiwa, a woman murdered by poisoning and despair, returns to avenge herself against her cruel husband, the idle *samurai* Iemon. Director Nakagawa employs his customary painterly visual style to conjure bleak and nightmarish visions of madness and the terrifying female phantasms which would haunt the Japanese horror film thereafter. There have been more than thirty film versions of *Tokaido yotsuya kaidan*; other notable versions that came later include Shiro Toyoda's gorier **Yotsuya kaidan** (1965) and Kazuo Mori's **Yotsuya kaidan Oiwa no borei** (1969).

LES YEUX SANS VISAGE
("Eyes Without A Face")
Production: France, 1959
Director: Georges Franju
Category: Horror

The classic film of surgical horror, which inspired a whole succession of similar entries centred around deranged doctors or plastic surgeons bent on skinning or disfiguring as many victims as possible in pursuit of their various ends. **Les Yeux Sans Visage** remains far superior to its many successors, a black and white art film in which the director conjures visual poetry from the most grim and disturbing subject matter. Dr Gessenier (Pierre Brasseur) is abducting young girls from whom to take skin grafts to restore the disfigured face of his daughter (played with exquisite melancholy by Edith Scob), who spends most of the film prowling their house behind an expressionless white mask. The scene of one these grafts being prepared, the skin peeled bloodily in clear close-up from the face of a "donor", was shocking for its time and led to the film being heavily censored in Britain and America (where it was ludicrously re-titled **Horror Chamber Of Dr Faustus**). Finally, the daughter rebels and in a double murder first stabs her nurse (Alida Valli) and then abandons her father to the savage, vengeful jaws of his laboratory dogs. Between these three bloody moments, Franju shows contrasting scenes of sombre beauty. Whether the film, like the director's previous abattoir documentary **Le Sang Des Betes** (1948), is ultimately meant as an anti-vivisectionist tract, is open to debate; what is clear is that Franju has bequeathed us a unique, transcendent work of twilit horror.

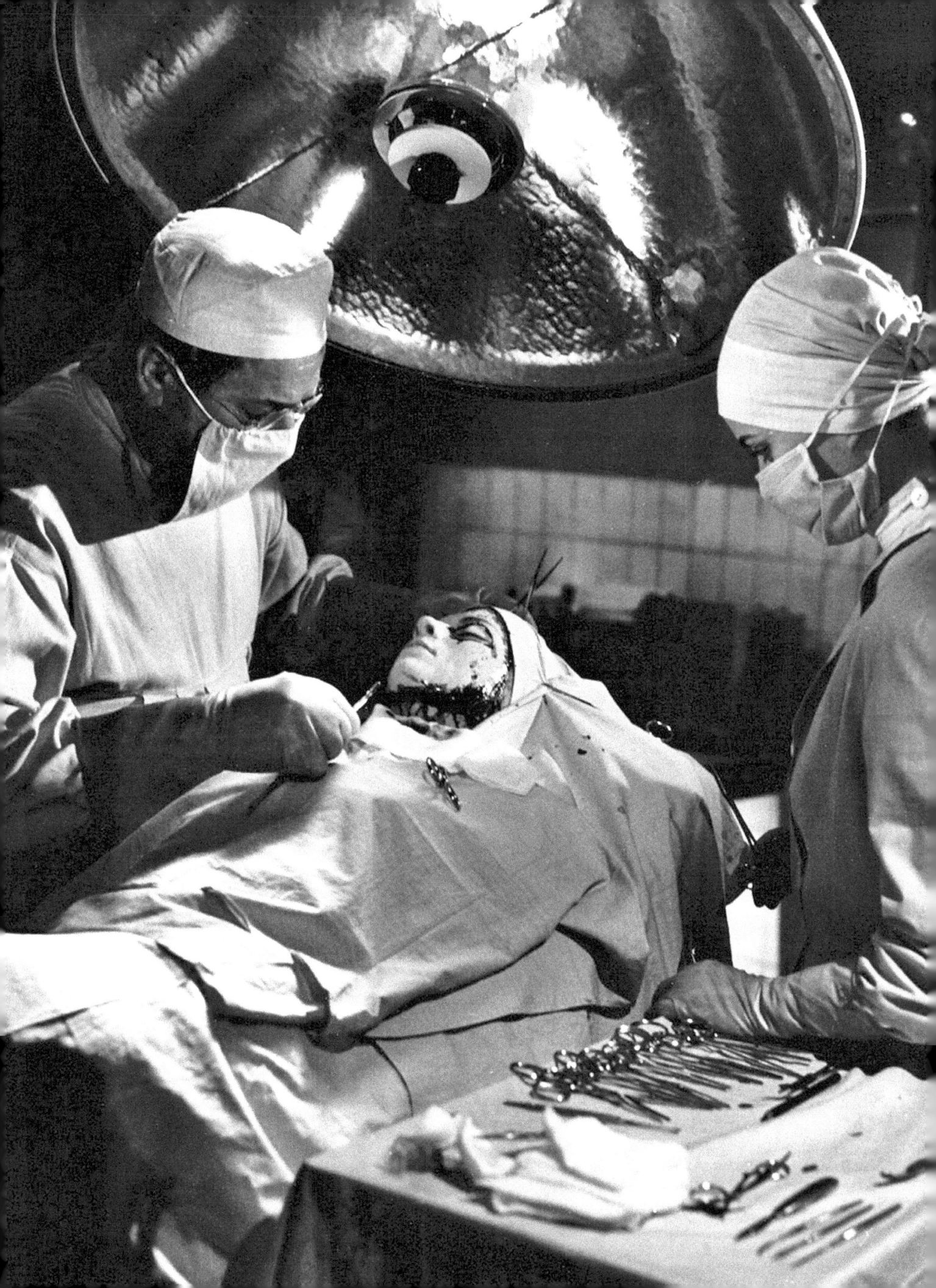

THE GIRL IN BLACK STOCKINGS
Production: USA, 1957
Director: Howard W. Koch
Category: Murder

MAYHEM

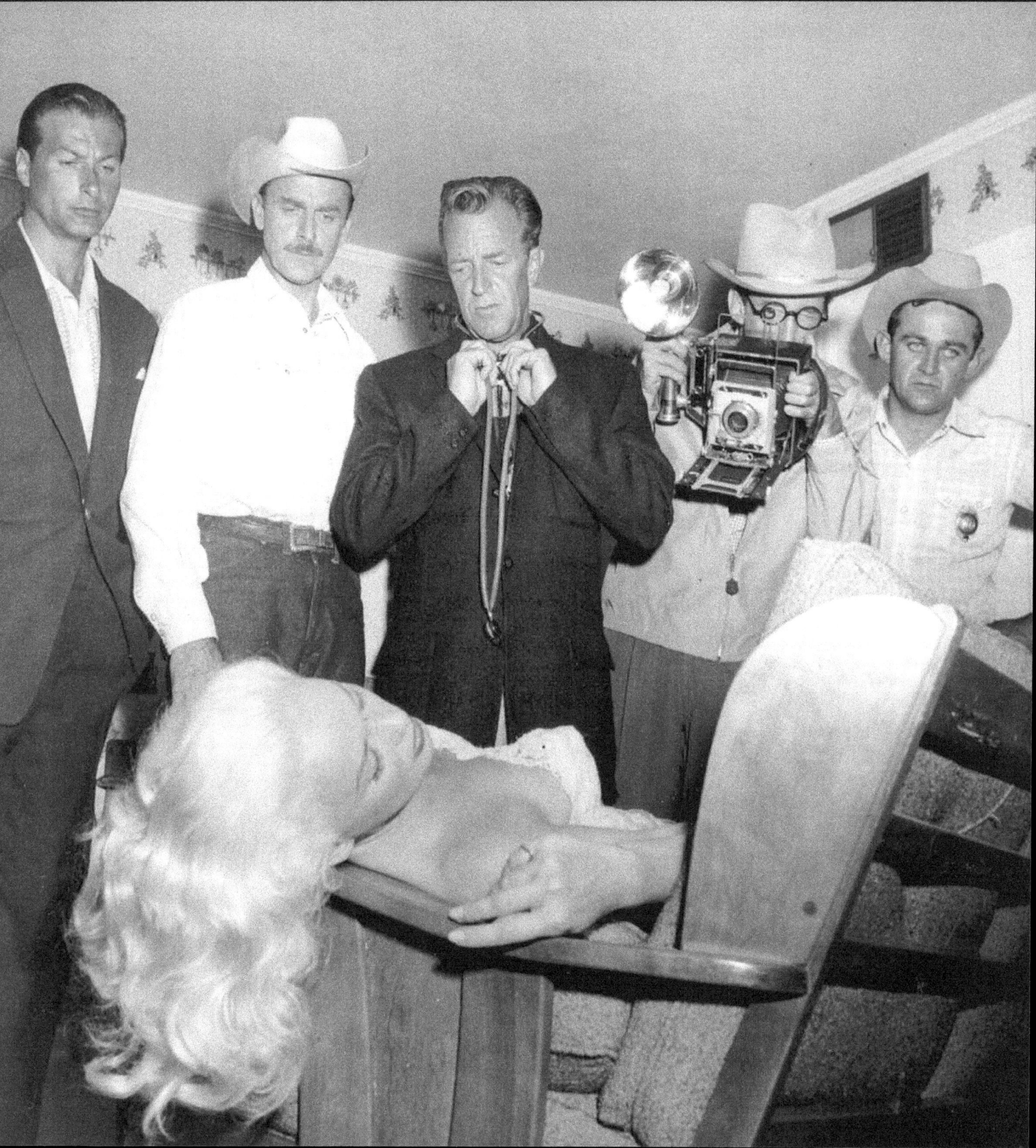

DEATH IN SMALL DOSES
Production: USA, 1957
Director: Joseph M. Newman
Category: Drugs/Beat Movement

The rise of the Beat generation in the 1950s was marked by a slew of films dealing with the sub-culture it promoted of drugs, jazz, wild parties and easy sex. One of the key Beat tropes, as outlined in novels like John Clellon Holmes' *Go* (1952) and Jack Kerouac's *On The Road* (1957), was movement, often expressed by the freedom of the open road and an amphetamine-fuelled velocity with which to exploit it. In **Death In Small Doses**, Chuck Connors plays Mink, a long-distance truck driving hepcat who drives for days on end without sleep due to the huge amount of bop pills he pops along the way. Jazz-loving, hip-speaking Mink lives life on the edge, and epitomises the popular notion of a speed junkie. Connors had previously appeared in a cautionary classroom film on juvenile delinquency, **Boy With A Knife** (1956). Amphetamine abuse was the latest focus of drugsploitation cinema in the late 50s, a genre which had previously devoted itself primarily to booze, cocaine, marijuana and opiates. A growing problem amongst teenagers popping barbiturates, benzedrine and other stimulants in pharmaceutical form led to the release of the first anti-pill educational film for schools, **Seduction Of The Innocent**, in 1961, and the problem continued to be addressed into the 70s, with films like **The Pill-Poppers** from 1971.

GUNS DON'T ARGUE
Production: USA, 1957
Director: Richard C. Kahn, Bill Karn
Category: Crime

A composite film made up from three episodes of the 1952 TV crime series **Gangbusters**, a docu-drama that lauded the FBI's battle against dangerous criminals in the 1920s and 1930s. Outlaws portrayed include Ma Barker, Bonnie And Clyde, John Dillinger, and Alvin Karpis. Co-director Karn's **Gang-Busters** (1955) was also a spin-off, but a slower-paced original.

DIE HALBSTARKEN
("The Teenagers")
Production: Germany, 1957
Director: Georg Tressler
US release title: **Teenage Wolf Pack**
Category: Juvenile Delinquency

HELL ON DEVIL'S ISLAND
Production: USA, 1957
Director: Christian Nyby
Category: Prison

HOT ROD RUMBLE
Production: USA, 1957
Director: Leslie H. Martinson
Category: Hot Rods/Juvenile Delinquency

MOTORCYCLE GANG
Production: USA, 1957
Director: Edward L. Cahn
Category: Biker/Juvenile Delinquency

A JD/biker movie about illegal street-racing, released after the sensational screen outburst of Marlon Brando's **The Wild One** in 1953 – which also prompted **Double-Cross** (1941), an old police thriller about renegade cycle cops, to be retitled **Motorcycle Squad** and re-released for television – and the meteoric rise/death of James Dean. **Motorcycle Gang** is just one of the many youth-oriented movies directed by veteran Cahn in the latter 1950s. It was followed in 1958 by films such as **Dragstrip Riot,** in which bikers clash with hot-rodders.

NACHTS, WENN DER TEUFEL KAM
("At Night, When the Devil Comes")
Production: Germany, 1957
Director: Robert Siodmak
US release title: **The Devil Strikes At Night**
Category: Crime/Serial Killer

Siodmak's first film upon returning to Germany was inspired by the case of Bruno Luedke, the mentally retarded serial killer who began to kill aged eighteen, and racked up some eighty rape/murder victims. During WW2, a chaotic time facilitating his murderous activities, he was arrested for a sexual offence and sterilised by order of the SS. But this did not weaken his homocidal instincts, and he went on killing unnoticed. When in January 1943 an elderly woman was found strangled in a Berlin forest, the police interrogated all registered criminals. Luedke was among them, and confessed after brutally attacking his captors. After investigating the relevant cases for one year, experts agreed that Luedke had been the murderer in almost all of them. The SS decided to cover up the case; Luedke was taken to a Viennese hospital where he was abused as a medical guinea pig in Nazi experiments, and died from the after-effect of an injection in April 1944. Siodmak's bleak film follows these events closely, conveying the horror of a system where individual freedoms or justice have no meaning. In the end, the direct comparison between Luedke's murder spree and the merciless meshings of the SS extermination camps is unavoidable.

TEENAGE DOLL
Production: USA, 1957
Director: Roger Corman
Category: Juvenile Delinquents/Girl Gangs
Although Roger Corman specialised in SF and horror movies during the early years of his career, he also produced several juvenile delinquent drama, of which **Teenage**

Doll is the outstanding example. That same year Corman also directed **Sorority Girl,** the tale of a sociopathic teenager, and **Rock All Night,** in which a group of night-clubbing beatniks are menaced by two armed thugs.

ASCENSEUR POUR L'ECHAFAUD
("Elevator To The Gallows")
Production: France, 1958
Director: Louis Malle
Category: Crime Noir

Malle's first feature film as director (he was previously a cinematographer for Jacques Cousteau) meshes proto-*Nouvelle Vague* stylings to the deconstructionist *film noir* protocols already set in motion that decade by Jean-Pierre Melville's **Bob Le Flambeur** (1956). Malle's tale of adultery, murder and the mundane is marked by Henri Decaë's experimental camera and, especially, by a phenomenal jazz score by Miles Davis – reputedly improvised during a single, heroin-driven nocturnal session – that mainlines directly into the evil beauty of night. (Malle's affinity with be-bop had already been demonstrated by the title of his first short film, the absurdist **Crazeology** [1953], named after a piece by Charlie Parker.) Malle's next film, **Les Amants,** brought his work to the attention of ordinary American movie-goers hoping for a glimpse of Jeanne Moreau's naked breasts.

THE BONNIE PARKER STORY
Production: USA, 1958
Director: William Witney
Category: Crime

When her husband is sentenced to 175 years behind bars and she is left all alone in the hard depression times, waitress Bonnie [Parker] transforms into a female gangster more than equal to her male counterparts in roughness and brutality. She learns to handle machine-guns and to kill without batting an eyelash, together with her new boyfriend Clyde Barrow (here called Guy Darrow). This sleazy, violent black-and-white crime saga deals very freely with the real story, but its brutal and pitiless characters are much closer to the real Bonnie and Clyde than the teenage-idols of Arthur Penn's later portrait. Here Bonnie Parker is no victim blindfolded by love, but rather a cigar-puffing, big-bosomed killer-blonde representing the dominant part of the legendary duo. Whipped by a pulsating score in the midst of cheap filthy scenery, she machine-guns a bloody swathe through this beautifully immoral B-movie.

THE CAMP ON BLOOD ISLAND
Production: USA, 1958
Director: Val Guest
Category: Prisoner-of-War/Atrocity
Early Hammer Films production, a war film depicting the brutal atrocities of the Japanese against their English prisoners. Its less apologetic tone in presenting scenes of cruelty and abuse was a welcome change at the time. A sequel of sorts, **The Secret Of Blood Island**, came in 1965. A novelisation of **Camp On Blood Island** – itself influenced by Lord Russell's illustrated war crimes exposé *Knights Of Bushido* – was Hammer's most reprinted film tie-in.

THE COOL AND THE CRAZY
Production: USA, 1958
Director: William Witney
Category: Drugs/Juvenile Delinquency
A classic drugs movie, in which a high-school rebel gets his class-mates high on marijuana. Produced by AIP, doyens of youthsploitation, this epitomises their 50s formula of rock and roll culture, teenage gang violence, substance abuse and sexy young girls in tight sweaters. Witney, formerly one of the great serial directors, next shot **Young And Wild** and **Juvenile Jungle**, both from the same year, which were distributed on a double-bill by Republic Pictures, eager to jump on the JD bandwagon.

COP HATER
Production: USA, 1958
Director: William Berke
Category: Crime/Maniac

THE CRY BABY KILLER
Production: USA, 1958
Director: Jus Addis
Category: Crime

This Corman production features a young Jack Nicholson in his first ever feature film role as a confused delinquent who accidentally shoots another youth during an argument and then takes hostage a mother and baby. Possibly influenced by the then-recent Charles Starkweather case (as indicated by its tagline: "Yesterday a teenage rebel, today a mad dog slayer!"), but also part of a growing wave of violent JD crime films such as **Mad At The World** (1955), the Ed Wood-scripted **The Violent Years** (1956, with teenage female man-rapers), or the Ed Wood co-scripted **Anatomy Of A Psycho** (1961).

GIRLS ON THE LOOSE
Production: USA, 1958
Director: Paul Henreid
Category: Crime/Bad Girls
Girl-gang mania as gun-crazy jezebels kill each other after a bank heist. From AIP.

HIGH SCHOOL CONFIDENTIAL
Production: USA, 1958
Director: Jack Arnold
Category: Juvenile Delinquency

Something of a departure for SF doyen Arnold, director of the classic **Incredible Shrinking Man** and several others in the genre, **High School Confidential** remains the most substantial entry in the new cycle of "teenage" movies that started in the late 1950s, films dealing with the problems of sex, violence, fast cars, and drugs amongst America's young. The film starts with live footage of Jerry Lee Lewis playing the title song in the back of a flatbed; Arnold goes on to present a pacy tale of high school drug-dealing, violence and promiscuity. Among the main attractions is actress Mamie van Doren, also seen in **Running Wild** and many other cine-tales of flaming youth. Unhappy about **High School Confidential**'s "immoral" ending – grinning drug-dealer drives into the sunset with two blondes – the Federal Narcotics Bureau made producer Albert Zugsmith cover this scene with a "square-up" text about the dangers of marijuana. Like fellow director William Witney, Jack Arnold split his directorial activities into different genres; best-known for SF, he combined that genre with the JD film to produce **Monster On The Campus** (also 1958), in which a science professor regresses to a primitive, half-human state. Other (less accomplished) JD films in the same mould included **High School Hellcats** (AIP, 1958), **High School Big Shot** (Sparta, 1959), and **High School Caesar** (Marathon, 1960).

JOOBACHI
("Queen Bee")
Production: Japan, 1958-61
Director: Various
Category: Yakuza/Bad Girl

One of the most significant developments in Japanese exploitation cinema of the late 1950s, spear-headed by Shintoho Studios, was the introduction of films featuring racy, delinquent or violent females, such as Nobuo Nakagawa's **Dokufu Takahashi Oden** ("Evil Woman Oden Takahashi", 1958), the case study of a notorious female murderer. This direction led to the female *yakuza* series **Joobachi**, starring Naoko Kubo and Yoko Mihara. Films in this series were **Joobachi** (Tetsu Taguchi, 1958); **Joobachi no ikari** (Teruo Ishii, 1958); **Joobachi to Daigaku no Ryû** (Teruo Ishii, 1960); and **Joobachi no gyakushû** (Kôzô Uchida, 1961). These stories incorporated key elements of female criminality, prostitution, girl gangs, and girls in prison, laying the groundwork for a "bad girl" cinema to develop over the ensuing decade. During this early period, Toei corporation contributed two **Zubeko Tenshi** ("Bad Angel') films, starring Mitsue Komiya, to the emerging female *yakuza* market. Shintoho went bankrupt in 1961, mainly due to distribution problems.

JUVENILE JUNGLE
Production: USA, 1958
Director: William Witney
Category: Juvenile Delinquency
Part of a JD double-bill from Republic (the other half was **Young And Wild**), produced to cash in on the youthsploitation craze that had been ignited by the rise of rock and roll and the teen rebel films churned out by AIP.

MACHINE-GUN KELLY
Production: USA, 1958
Director: Roger Corman
Category: Crime
One of Corman's two contributions to the late 50s revival of the gangster movie – the other being **I, Mobster** from the same year – whose initial wave had peaked belatedly with **White Heat** in 1949. Following hard on the heels of Don Siegel's raw pulp blast **Baby Face Nelson** (1957), Corman's movie features Charles Bronson as Kelly, a small-time hoodlum with a crippling death phobia (he almost faints at the sight of coffins), dominated by his girlfriend Flo Becker, and a coward without the phallic power of his slug-spitting Thompson sub-machine-gun. This trend of emphasising gangsters' inadequacies peaked with the sexually impotent Clyde Barrow

in Arthur Penn's bloodbath **Bonnie And Clyde** (1967). Corman himself returned to the genre with the semi-documentary **The St Valentines Day Massacre,** also in 1967 – maybe the best film ever made about Al Capone – followed in 1970 by the white trash mania of **Bloody Mama,** starring Shelley Winters and featuring Robert de Niro in his first ever screen gangster role.

SAFETY OR SLAUGHTER
Production: Canada, 1958
Director: James Seymour
Category: Documentary/Auto-Mayhem
Driver educational film, notable for being among the first of its kind to insert gory footage of real car-crash deaths. A Budge Crawley production (Crawley was a pioneer of Canadian independent cinema, producing dozens of short films, feature films, television commercials, animated cartoons and other products in a long and acclaimed career). An early harbinger of car-crash culture, an American phenomenon which would later be quantfied by author J.G. Ballard in his seminal work *The Atrocity Exhibition.*

TOUCH OF EVIL
Production: USA, 1958
Director: Orson Welles
Category: Crime Noir

VERTIGO
Production: USA, 1958
Director: Alfred Hitchcock
Category: Psychological Thriller
A man is tormented by a phantasmic female, who may or may not be possessed by the spirit of a long-dead suicide. With its facets of sexual obsession, mania, phobia, murder and memory, **Vertigo** has often been cited as a key influence on the Italian *giallo* film, an extravagant psycho-crime genre which developed in the 1960s and ran riot in the 1970s.

THE BEAT GENERATION
Production: USA, 1959
Director: Charles F. Haas
US re-release title: **This Rebel Age**
Category: Beat Movement/Maniac

Beatsploitation movie, using the beat/coffee bar scene as a backdrop to the pursuit of a psychopathic rapist. It was produced by Albert Zugsmith, and features one of his regular actresses, the phenomenal Mamie Van Doren. TV horror hostess Vampira also does a turn as a beatnik poet. Another beat/murder fusion was **The Bloody Brood** (also 1959), with Peter Falk as a beatnik psycho, while **The Fat Black Pussycat** (1962) featured a string of girls murdered in the beatnik haunts of Greenwich Village by a psychotic lesbian.

BEAT GIRL
Director: Edmond T. Greville
Production: UK, 1959
US release title: **Wild For Kicks**
Category: Beat Movement

Beatsploitation came to England, too. Young art student rebels, acts outrageously by stripping at parties, driving too fast, playing with speeding trains. Oliver Reed makes a brief appearance, one of his very first, and Christopher Lee plays a sleazy Soho club owner. Like Don Chaffey's **The Flesh Is Weak** (1957, an "exposé" of prostitution and vice), **Beat Girl** is a classic British example of (muted) sleaze posing as social commentary. Other films set in Soho strip clubs included **Too Hot To Handle** (1960, starring Jayne Mansfield), **Jungle Street** (1961), and **Strip Tease Murder** (1961).

THE BIG OPERATOR
Production: USA, 1959
Director: Charles Haas
Category: Crime Noir
Gangster exploitationer enlivened by the presence of ultra-sex goddess Mamie Van Doren, and remarkable for its scenes of excessive (for the time) violence, including one man being set on fire and another hurled into a cement mixer, plus a lengthy torture sequence. That same year Van Doren could be seen causing mayhem in numerous productions including **Vice Raid, Girls Town,** and **Guns Girls And Gangsters.**

THE BLOODY BROOD
Production: USA/Canada, 1959
Director: Julian Roffman
Category: Crime/Beat Movement

COMPULSION
Production: USA, 1959
Director: Richard Fleischer
Category: True Crime

Compulsion is the second film to deal with the case of the 1920s "Thrill Killers", Nathan Leopold and Richard Loeb (the first was Hitchcock's stagey **Rope** of 1948). Leopold (19) and Richard Loeb (18) were the sons of millionaires, homosexuals, and advocates of Nietzschean philosophy. In order to prove Nietzsche's theory of the "superman", the lovers agreed to commit the "perfect" crime together. For a few years they committed minor larceny, arson, and similar malpractices, but in 1924 decided to kidnap someone, kill him, and go to Europe with the ransom (they did not need money, but would demand it only for the sake of credibility). For a victim they randomly chose 14-year-old Bobby Franks, taking the boy with them in a rented car. Leopold drove, and Loeb stabbed the boy four times with a chisel. It lasted fifteen minutes, until Bobby had finally bled to death. Afterwards the killers drove to an out-of-the-way swamp area, undressed the corpse, and hid it in a sewer-pipe. Then they posted the blackmailing letter. But Bobby was quickly found on the following day, and police also found Leopold's glasses on the scene of the crime. Only eight days after the murder, the boys were suspected of the deed and interrogated. The "strong" Loeb broke down first and confessed. The trial shook Chicago, and some people even called for a lynching, but the young men were defended by the famous lawyer Clarence Darrow, who argued against the death penalty citing Freud's then revolutionary theories about sexuality and childhood. For their youth and the confession of their guilt they were sentenced only to imprisonment for life, plus 99 years. **Compulsion**, shot in black-and-white, starts out with a racy exposition of the boys' twisted philosophy and sexuality, and then stops still for the trial (the actual murder is not shown). The trial sequence remains notable for the performance of Orson Welles as Darrow, delivering an eloquent and passionate speech on behalf of his young clients (played by Dean Stockwell and Bradford Dillman). Director Fleischer seemed drawn to true crime cases; he went on to make **The Boston Strangler** and **10 Rillington Place** (about English mass-murderer John Reginald Christie), and all three films stand out in his otherwise largely mediocre portfolio.

COVER GIRL KILLER
Production: UK, 1959
Director: Terry Bishop
Category: Crime/Maniac
A daring film for England at the time, featuring a sexually-frustrated, voyeuristic psycho-killer preying on bikini-clad cover girls. The killer spouts some great pseudo-profound lines about "liberating man from lustful images" and "sex and horror as the new gods" as he goes about his murderous business. At around one hour in duration, **Cover Girl Killer** would have made a great support for its contemporary, **Peeping Tom**. Distributed by Butchers Film Service of Soho.

DER FROSCHE MIT DER MASKE
("The Frog With The Mask")
Production: Germany, 1959
Director: Harald Reinl
Category: Krimi
In 1950s Germany, a growing craze for pulp crime novels, known as *taschenkrimis*, led to a similar popularity in garish mystery movies – such as 1954's **Das Phantom Des Großen Zeltes** – which became known as *krimis*. Hoping to cash in on this market, and inspired by the 1952 UK production of Edgar Wallace's **The Ringer**, the Rialto film company struck up a licensing deal to make films of Wallace's novels and stories, starting in 1959 with **Der Frosche Mit Der Maske** (based on the novel *The Fellowship Of The Frog*, which had previously been filmed as a 10-part UK serial, **Mark Of The Frog**, in 1928, and again in 1937 as **The Frog**). London is terrorized by a criminal gang who sport frog tattoos and leave the body parts of frogs at the scene of their iniquities, and whose leader hides his identity behind a bulbous amphibian mask. Due to their pulp elements of horror, sadism, the macabre and the grotesque, *krimis* based on or inspired by Edgar Wallace soon acquired their own sub-genre – the *gruselkrimi*. Rialto followed up with **Der Rote Kreis**, (1959) a new version of Wallace's novel *The Crimson Circle*, and went on to produce another thirty titles in the series, which finally ended with 1972's German-Italian *gruselkrimi-giallo* hybrid **Sette Orchidee Macchiate Di Rosso**.

GUNS GIRLS AND GANGSTERS
Production: USA, 1959
Director: Edward L. Cahn
Category: Crime

THE HORRORS OF THE BLACK MUSEUM
Production: UK, 1959
Director: Arthur Crabtree
Category: Mayhem/Murder
A sadistic film which concerns a journalist (Michael Gough) who commits a series of bloody murders to satisfy his readers. His increasingly sadistic methods include the use of "trick" binoculars which gouge out the user's eyes with spring-loaded spikes, and a guillotine/bed device which decapitates a voluptuous prostitute. This was the first British "serial killer" film produced by American Herman Cohen, formerly with AIP. He worked with Gough again on the misguided giant ape flick **Konga**, and then took the actor back to the States to act in films like **Black Zoo** (1963). Cohen returned to the UK in 1967 and produced **Beserk!**.

JACK THE RIPPER
Production: UK, 1959
Director: Robert S. Baker
Category: Mayhem/Murder
Baker and his partner, Monty Berman, were prolific producers of both films and television series; **Jack The Ripper** was one of the more macabre of their creations for the cinema (which also included **The Hellfire Club**, **The Flesh And The Fiends**, and **Blood Of The Vampire**), but remains tame compared to certain films of that period from countries other than England.

LA MUJER Y LA BESTIA
("The Woman And The Beast")
Production: Mexico, 1959
Director: Alfonso Corona Blake
Category: Mayhem/Murder
An exploitational production concerning a nurse with a split personality, who by night turns into a psychopathic prostitute murdering men with a meathook.

NAZARÍN
Production: Spain, 1959
Director: Luis Buñuel
Category: Crime
Another manifestation of Buñuel's equation of poverty and squalor with physical abnormality, in a tale of prostitution, murder and insanity.

PEEPING TOM
Production: UK, 1959
Director: Michael Powell
Category: Mayhem/Maniac
The film which effectively ended Powell's illustrious career, **Peeping Tom** features Karl Boehm as Mark, a photographer obsessed with physical flaws and scars. He is also psychopathic, and kills his female models while he is filming them by means of an extending spike affixed to his camera tripod. It turns out that Mark was the victim of similar experiments by his father, who filmed him relentlessly and subjected him to fright and suffering in order to record his reactions. With its unusually complex structure and layers of symbolism, **Peeping Tom** is without doubt the ultimate statement on the voyeuristic nature of the whole cinematic experience. The viewer

not only watches films within films, but is made to experience the very act of film-making – and murder – subjectively while still acutely aware that he is being manipulated into this complicity by his relationship with the film-makers (Mark/Mark's father/Powell). Mark's choice of victims (tarts, models, actresses – one of whom is played by famous nude model Pamela Green) are all girls routinely scrutinized and objectified in their "glamorous" careers; by means of a large mirror mounted on his camera, Mark conveys the ultimate irony, forcing them to watch their own death throes as he impales them. He finally falls for a plain girl (Anna Massey), but her blind mother – the only one immune from this inwardly-collapsing gaze maze – is suspicious of him and engineers his downfall. Nude scenes with Green were incorporated in overseas versions of the film, which was universally reviled upon release – a disaster for Powell (who to top things off plays the part of Mark's father in the "home movies"), and it virtually ruined him. It has since been critically rehabilitated to its rightful status as a masterpiece.

THE PURPLE GANG
Production: USA, 1959
Director: Frank McDonald
Category: Crime

The Purple Gang (so named because they were "rotten", the colour of bad meat) were a vicious and ultra-violent gang of bootleggers operating out of Detroit during Prohibition; led by one Abe Bernstein, they are believed to have slaughtered over five hundred rival gang members during their reign of terror, which ended with internecine violence in 1932.

SIGNAL 30
Production: USA, 1959
Director: Richard Wayman
Category: Documentary/Auto-Mayhem

30-minute driver educational film; "Signal 30" is official Ohio State Highway Patrol code for a road fatality, and these are shown in graphic detail. Corpses burnt beyond recognition, crushed torsos, impalement, all voiced-over with strong admonitions against the dangers of the road (cars are described as "motorized coffins"), were the shock formula which sought to scare teenager drivers into models of caution. **Signal 30** was the first in a notorious trilogy of gory driver films which continued with Wayman's **Mechanized Death** (1961) and **Wheels Of Tragedy** (1963). This approach to driver safety can be dated as far back as **Last Date** (1950), in which a teenage girl accepts a ride from a reckless youth and ends up hideously disfigured by a crash.

LES TRIPES AU SOLEIL
("Guts In The Sun")
Production: France, 1959
Director: Claude Bernard-Albert
US release title: **Checkerboard**
Category: Violence

Very odd French imagining of a race-segregated town in the southern states of America, with images of drink-sodden hicks spoiling for a lynching in a seedy run-down hell-hole where kids kick human skulls around. The same director made **Les Lâches Vivent D'Espoir** (1961, about a mixed-race baby) before progressing to porn films with Brigitte Lahaie in the 70s. Another French vision of American racism and violence was **J'Irai Cracher Sur Vos Tombes**, directed by Michel Gast that same year.

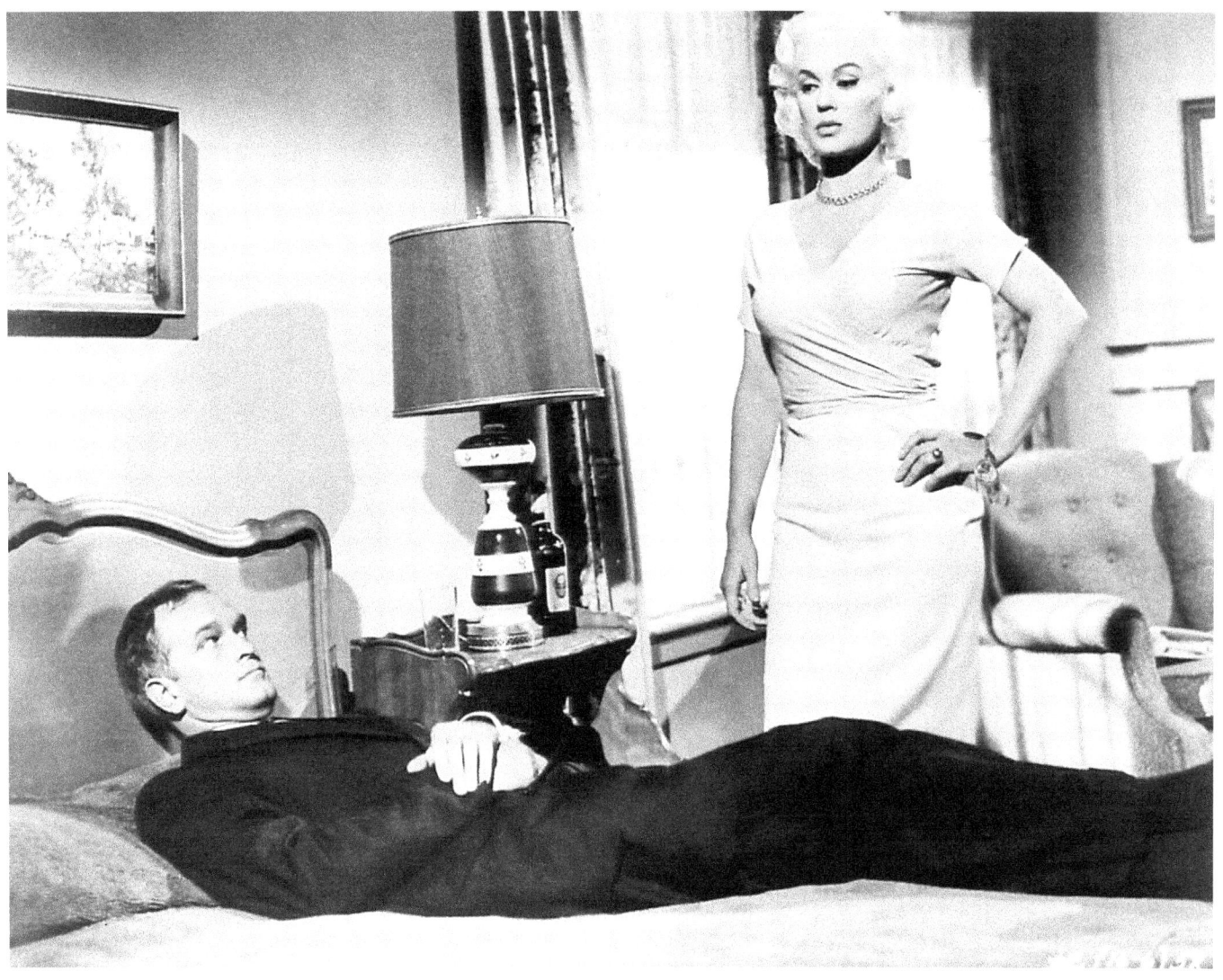

VICE RAID
Production: USA, 1959
Director: Edward L. Cahn
Category: Crime/Prostitution

THE LAND UNKNOWN
Production: USA, 1957
Director: Virgil W. Vogel
Category: Lost Worlds

MYTH

THE ABOMINABLE SNOWMAN
Production: UK, 1957
Director: Val Guest
Category: Myth

Hammer version of the Yeti legend, with Peter Cushing, and scripted by Nigel Kneale from his original BBC play. A scientist and a fortune-seeking hunter come into conflict over the mythical beast as both stalk it, for different reasons, across the snow-covered Himalayas. Telepathic monks also feature in this intelligent and occasionally eerie film. Japanese company Toho had actually produced their own, equally convincing Yeti movie, **Jujin Yuki Otoko,** two years before, and in 1958 this was bought by US producer who recut and dubbed it, adding footage of American actors (including John Carradine), and released it under the new title **Half Human: The Story Of The Abominable Snowman**. Unfortunately, the original movie was suppressed in Japan for political reasons, and remains unscreened since it first came out. The worst Yeti film in terms of special effects may be W. Lee Wilder's **Snow Creature** (1954), but when the monster is half-glimpsed in dark alleys or – the best sequence – blundering through racks of slaughterhouse carcasses, Wilder achieves a few effective moments. Jerry Warren's **Man Beast** (1955) was an equally low-budget effort promising "women stalked and captured for breeding by Yeti monsters", while **El Monstruo De Los Volcanes** ("Monster From The Volcano") and **El Terrible Gigante De Las Nieves** ("The Terrible Snow Giant", both directed by Jaime Salvador in 1963) were a cheap Mexican attempt at the legend, in which the Yeti inhabits an extinct volcano.

EL JINETE SIN CABEZA
("The Rider With No Head")
Production: Mexico, 1957
Director: Chano Urueta
Category: Weird Western

A film which plays of the legend of the headless horseman. Townsfolk terrorized by a murderous cult of Skull-masked predators, whose icon is a severed hand that seemingly has a life of its own, are rescued by a mysterious rider who they believe has no head. This horseman soon returned in two weird-tinged sequels, **La Marca De Satanás** and **La Cabeza De Pancho Villa**, both again directed by Urueta in 1957.

KUMONOSU-JO
("Spider-Web Castle")
Production: Japan, 1957
Director: Akira Kurosawa
English release title: **Throne Of Blood**
Category: Chambara

Akira Kurosawa's highly stylized **Kumonosu-jo** is his version of *Macbeth*, featuring a traditional *Noh* chorus narrative, *Noh* stagings, and fetishized make-up resembling *Noh* masks. Allied to scenes of feudal violence and witchcraft, this staging elevates the original play in a new artistic fusion, further enhamced by the specal effects of Eiiji Tsuburaya. *Chambara* star Toshiro Mifune plays Macbeth/Washizu, slain in a hail of arrows. *Noh* theatre originally developed from travelling fairs, and its present form derives from the player Zeami Motokiyo (1362-1443). It is a highly encrypted art form, relying on symbolism, allusion and body language to convey complex themes. *Noh* elements have rarely been incorporated into film, but another example of note is Masaki Kobayashi's **Kwaidan**, a ghost story whose spectres all have *Noh* correlatives.

THE BRIDE AND THE BEAST
Production: USA, 1958
Director: Adrian Weiss
Category: Jungle Exploitation/Gorilla

Perhaps the last great work in a long-running thread of prurient trash cinema dealing with implied human/gorilla miscegeny, **The Bride And The Beast** was apparently concocted in order to utilize an acquired cache of stock jungle footage (mainly taken from the 1948 killer tiger classic **Man-Eater Of Kumaon**). Z-movie maverick Edward Wood Jr. was engaged to drum up a script, and delivered a typically weird scenario (possibly inspired by Curt Siodmak's 1951 **Bride Of The Gorilla**) in which a man's wife experiences an inexplicable sexual attraction to his pet gorilla (named Spanky); hypnotic regression ultimately reveals that in a former life she was herself an ape, none other than the Gorilla Queen. Weiss embellishes the tale with bizarre dream sequences, and Wood ends on a twisted note as the woman is snatched by another bull ape and disappears (not unwillingly) to her fate.

LE FATICHE DI ERCOLE
("The Toils Of Hercules")
Production: Italy, 1958
Director: Pietro Francisi
Category: Myth/Peplum
The film which launched the phenomenon of the peplum, or "sword-and-sandal" film genre, consisting mainly of narratives based on ancient history and myth. American body-builder Steve Reeves plays Ercole (Hercules), and would return in a sequel entitled **Ercole E La Regina Di Lidia** (1959), known in English as **Hercules Unchained**.

THE SEVENTH VOYAGE OF SINBAD
Production: USA, 1958
Director: Nathan Juran
Category: Myth
The first fantasy film to fully showcase the animation brilliance of Ray Harryhausen, and the first in a series of mythological stories he would work on over the ensuing

decades, creating creatures and beasts for a range of subjects ranging from **Jason And The Argonauts** to Hammer's remake of **One Million Years BC**. **The Seventh Voyage Of Sinbad** is famous not only for its cyclops, snake woman, and sword-fighting skeleton, but also for its sustained ambience of phantasmagoric exotica. In 1969, experimental film-maker Mike Jacobsen constructed a cut-up of Juran's original film, running at 45 minutes and in three eye-popping sections, entitled **Loop Variations From The Seventh Voyage Of Sinbad**, confirming the films' inherent psychedelic possibilities. Harryhausen eventually produced two sequels, **The Golden Voyage Of Sinbad** (1973) and **Sinbad And The Eye Of The Tiger** (1977).

TERROR IN A TEXAS TOWN
Production: USA, 1958
Director: Joseph H. Lewis
Category: Western
Lewis's last film, a bizarre western which climaxes in a showdown between a black-clad, metal-handed gunslinger and a Swedish seaman brandishing a whaling harpoon.

THE WILD WOMEN OF WONGO
Production: USA, 1958
Director: James L. Wolcott
Category: Fantasy

ERCOLE E LA REGINA DI LIDIA
("Hercules And The Queen Of Lidia")
Production: USA, 1959
Director: Pietro Francisci
US release title: **Hercules Unchained**
Category: Myth/Peplum

JUNGFRUKÄLLAN
("The Virgin Spring")
Production: Sweden, 1959
Director: Ingmar Bergman
Category: Historical/Violence
Bleak and violent (for its time) prototype of Wes Craven's **Last House On The Left**. Set in mediaeval times, Bergman's black-and-white film carries an undiminished primal charge as it unfurls a tale of rape, murder, and blood-curdling revenge.

SAMPO
Production: Finland, 1959
Director: Aleksandr Ptushko
US release title: **The Day The Earth Froze**
Category: Myth

THE STRANGLERS OF BOMBAY
Production: UK, 1959
Director: Terence Fisher
Category: Historical/Death Cults

Stranglers Of Bombay turned out to be Hammer Films' most brutal, notoriously sadistic movie up to that point. The story is set in India in 1826 and deals with the cult of *thugee* which erupted when worshippers of the death-goddess Kali began robbing, strangling and often mutilating thousands of victims, interring them in mass graves and undermining the authority of the British East India Company. Huge-breasted Marie Devereux plays Kali's handmaiden and agent of destruction. Eventually the secret organisation is broken up, but not before we see such horrors as blindings, evisceration, decapitations and (implied) castration.

THE INVISIBLE BOY
Production: USA, 1957
Director: Herman Hoffman
Category: Science Fiction

SCI-FI

THE AMAZING COLOSSAL MAN
Production: USA, 1957
Director: Bert I. Gordon
Category: Science Fiction

Amazing indeed, a psychedelic onslaught in which an army colonel exposed to radiation mutates to giant proportions, and finally launches an attack on Las Vegas wearing only diapers. Gordon's 1958 sequel, the brilliantly-titled **War Of The Colossal Beast**, added facial disfigurement to ramp up the horror quotient.

THE ASTOUNDING SHE MONSTER
Production: USA, 1957
Director: Ronald V. Ashcroft
Category: Science Fiction
A female space invader is battled by crooks and a scientist; the sexy alien (played by Shirley Kilpatrick, a stripper) is blonde and clad in a skin-tight metallic catsuit and high heels (the film's shooting title was **The Naked Invader**). This image of the seductive, sadistic and fetishized female would persist into the SF films of the 60s.

ATTACK OF THE CRAB MONSTERS
Production: USA, 1957
Director: Roger Corman
Category: Horror

Perhaps the most engaging of the early Corman SF films to feature strange creatures; atomic mutation causes crabs to grow to gigantic proportions and stalk human prey, decapitating their victims and assimilating their intelligence by devouring their brains. Another giant sea-creature featured in Corman's **The Saga Of The Viking Women And Their Voyage To The Waters Of The Great Sea Serpent** from the same year; both films were shot in the same locations, principally Bronson Caves in Los Angeles. **Attack Of The Crab Monsters** was the first entry in the giant killer crab genre that would later include Hammer's **The Lost Continent** (1965) and **When Dinosaurs Ruled The Earth** (1970), amongst others.

THE BLACK SCORPION
Production: USA, 1957
Director: Edward Ludwig
Category: Science Fiction/Giant Bug
Of all the over-sized attackers in 1950s giant creature movies, a scorpion might be the most horrific – at least in theory. In this not so well-known entry, giant scorpions are disturbed by a volcanic eruption and invade Mexico City, led by the biggest and blackest of them all. What really marks out **The Black Scorpion** from other monster films of the period is the brilliantly effective stop-motion animation by Willis O'Brien, creator of **King Kong**. O'Brien also animated a chilling sequence showing a descent into the volcano, where not only baby scorpions, but also other foul creatures like worms and spiders, await – a scene first conceived for **King Kong**, but unused. Only lack of budget, evident in the repetition of some sequences and the incomplete nature of some effects, spoils the film to a degree.

CHIKYU BOEIGUN
("Earth Defence Force")
Production: Japan, 1957
Director: Ishiro Honda
English release title: **The Mysterians**
Category: Science Fiction
Aliens from the ruined planet Mysteroid invade Earth (focusing on Japan) with the express purpose of capturing and raping human females in a bid to regenerate their

107

own decimated species. Mankind resists, sparking a colorful and strident blast of death-ray warfare. Director Honda and his regular special effects expert Eiji Tsuburaya also indulge their love of giant monsters by introducing Moguera, a huge robot raptor used by the aliens to terrorize and destroy. The US release, from RKO in 1959, featured an unusual set of hand-illustrated lobby cards, styled in the manner of bubblegum cards. (The art of bubblegum SF would peak a couple of years later with the release of the gory and sadistic Topps series *Mars Attacks* in 1962, which later inspired Tim Burton's inferior 1996 film homage of the same name.) **The Mysterians** was the first SF movie filmed in widescreen TohoScope, and the first Toho film to use Perspecta stereophonic sound. The original Japanese title means "Earth Defence Force". Honda followed up with **Uchu Daisenso** (1959), another Earth invasion movie (notable for its special effects of dogfighting spacecraft), and completed his unofficial "space apocalypse trilogy" with **Yosei Gorasu** (1962), in which a giant meteor is on collision course for mankind's beleaguered planet.

THE DEADLY MANTIS
Production: USA, 1957
Director: Nathan Juran
Category: Science Fiction/Giant Bug

One of the last, and best, of the giant creature movies of the 1950s. While not as deadly as a scorpion or spider, the mantis must be the nastiest of all insects, so it was a good choice. Here, a giant prehistoric specimen with a taste for fresh meat is awoken from its centuried artctic hibernation, and duly attacks civilisation. Director Juran thereafter specialized in SF movies, including the classic **Attack Of The 50 Foot Woman**.

FROM HELL IT CAME
Production: USA, 1957
Director: Dan Milner
Category: Science Fiction/Horror

THE INCREDIBLE SHRINKING MAN
Production: USA, 1957
Director: Jack Arnold
Category: Science Fiction

INVASION OF THE SAUCER MEN
Production: USA, 1957
Director: Edward L. Cahn
Category: Science Fiction

One of the weirdest of the 50s SF craze, directed by pulp master Cahn, with hideous bulb-headed aliens attacking American teenagers. As an added bonus, one of the saucer creatures is played by Angelito Rossitto, king of the exploitation movie dwarfs. Other dwarfs and/or midgets playing the aliens included Floyd Hugh Dixon and Edward Gibbons. **Invasion Of The Saucermen** was remade in 1965, under the new title **The Eye Creatures**, as a TV movie by Larry Buchanan. This came about because AIP wanted to break into the lucrative television licensing market, but were severely disadvantaged due to most of their classic SF films of the 50s being black and white. They therefore decided to hire Buchanan to remake several of the films in 16mm colour. **The Eye Creatures** turned out to be total low-budget trash, but at least it was colour trash. Buchanan's other AI-TV efforts were equally poor; they were: **Zontar: The Thing From Venus** (1966, a remake of **It Conquered The World**); **Curse Of The Swamp Creature** (1966, a remake of **Voodoo Woman**); **In The Year 2889** (1967, a remake of **The Day The World Ended**); and **Creature Of Destruction** (1967, a remake of **She Creature**). Buchanan also made **Mars Needs Women** (1967, possibly inspired by **Pajama Party**), and **It's Alive!** (1969, based on an unfilmed AIP script). Along with similar cheap efforts like the notorious **Creeping Terror** (Vic Savage, 1964), all of these rank amongst the absolute worst SF films of the 60s.

KRONOS
Production: USA, 1957
Director: Kurt Neumann
Category: Science Fiction

A low-budget, monochrome giant robot movie by Neumann, who four years later would make one of the all-time classics of tripped-out SF, **The Fly**. **Kronos** features some effective, weird stop-motion animation in its depiction of the colossal metallic space invader which threatens to drain the Earth of all its energy.

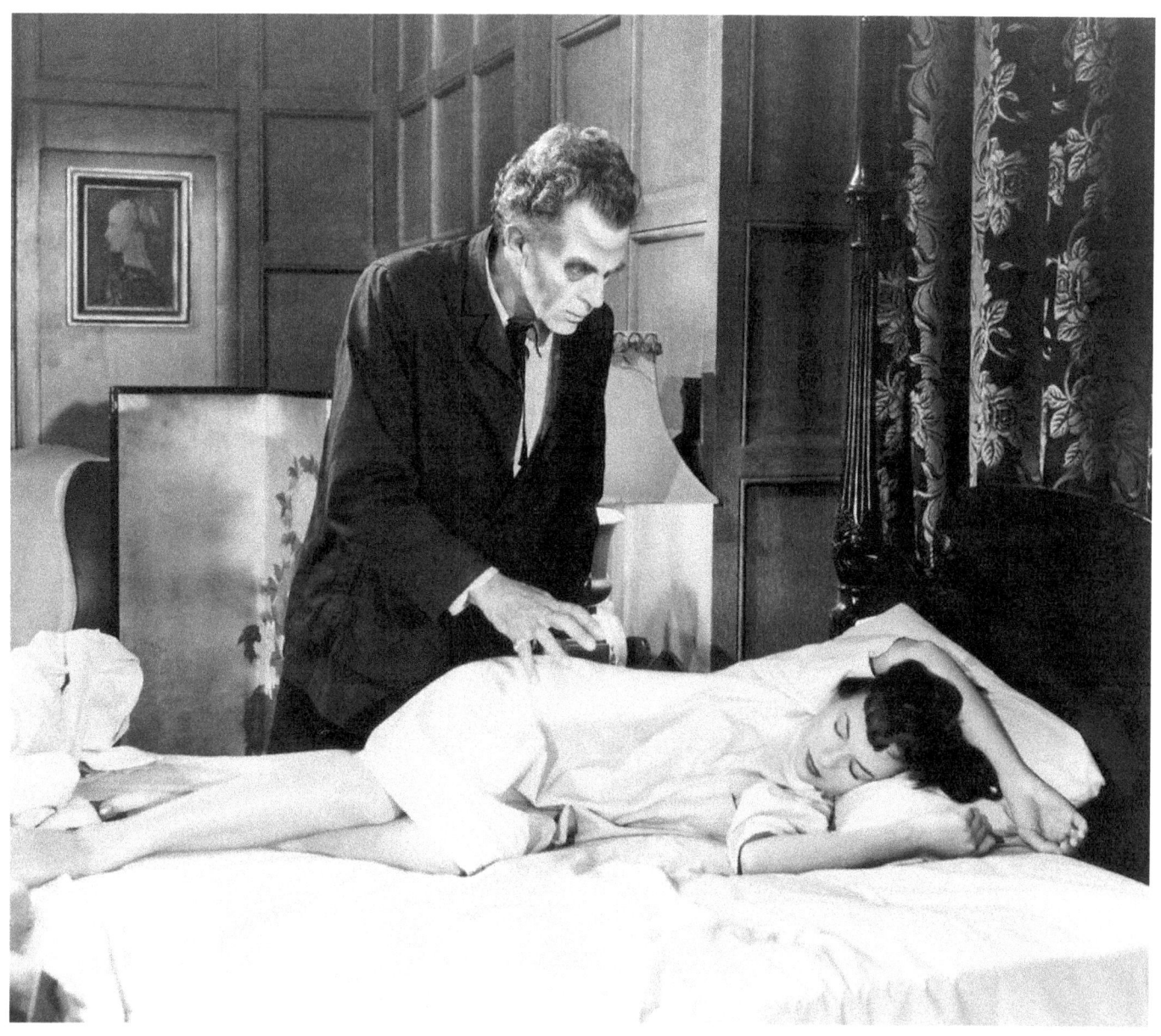

THE MAN WHO TURNED TO STONE
Production: USA, 1957
Director: Leslie Kardos
Category: Science Fiction/Horror

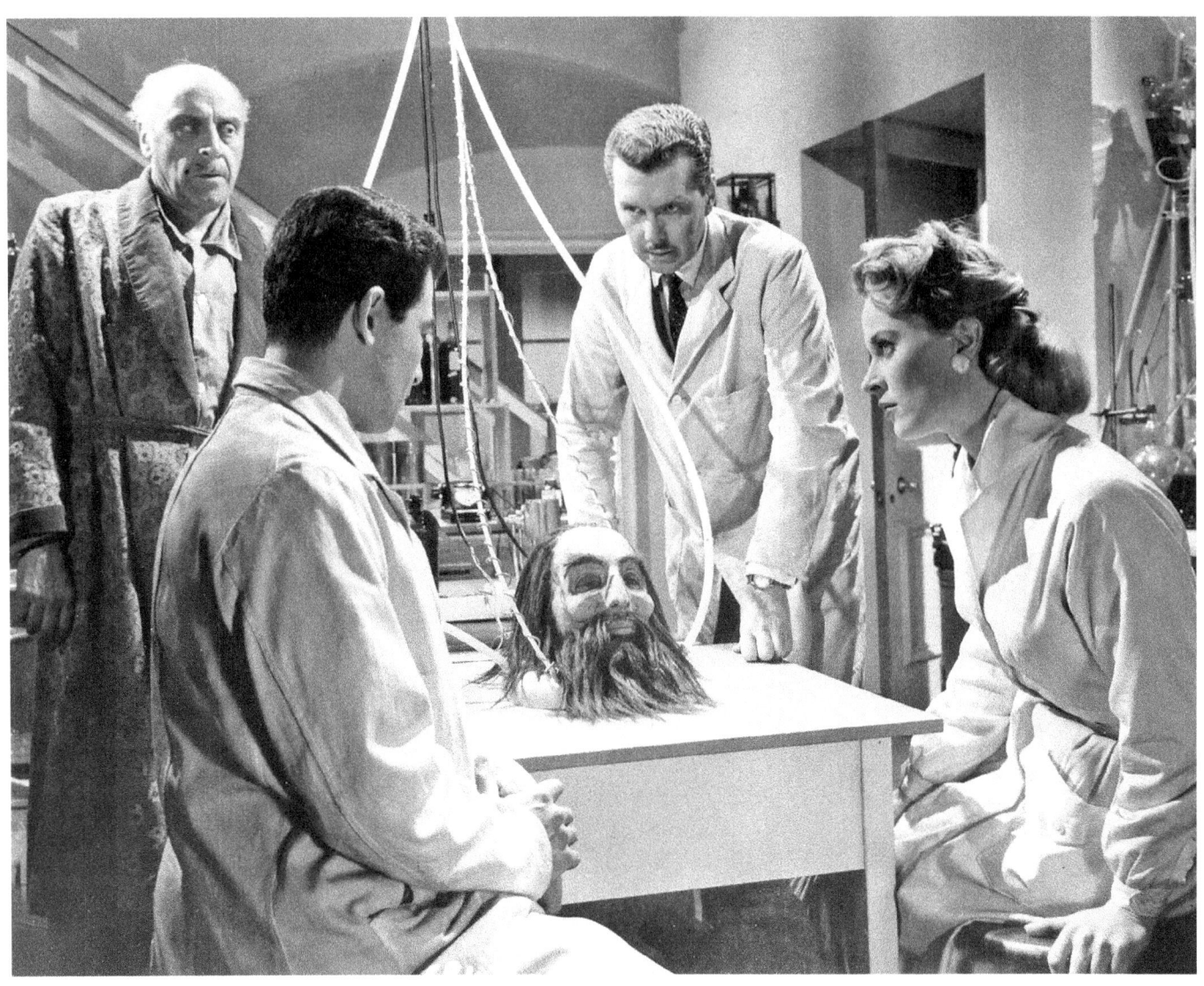

THE MAN WITHOUT A BODY
Production: UK, 1957
Director: W. Lee Wilder, Charles Saunders
Category: Science Fiction/Horror

One of the strangest films to emerge from the UK in the 1950s, one of numerous "living head" movies to surface during that period. Wilder, of Austro-Hungarian birth, emerged as a purveyor of low-budget but inventive SF in the early 50s with **Phantom From Space** (1953) and **Killers From Space** (1954). His **Manfish** (1956), despite being ostensibly an Edgar Allan Poe adaptation (blending elements of both "The Gold Bug" and "The Tell-Tale Heart") and starring Lon Chaney, Jr, was a mediocre deep-sea adventure devoid of the horror normally associated with that authorship.

THE MONOLITH MONSTERS
Production: USA, 1957
Director: John Sherwood
Category: Science Fiction

From a story by the great Jack Arnold, this low-budget SF thriller at least offers an original kind of threat to the planet; instead of the usual giant insects or arachnids, the monolith monsters are meteorite fragments which rapidly expand into black crystal when mixed with water, and also have the power to petrify humans. Growing to enormous sizes, they crash, shatter and then thrust upwards again like giant impaling devices. The film is also marked by some very potent and horrific imagery deriving from nightmarish juxtapositions of flesh and stone.

THE MONSTER FROM GREEN HELL
Production: USA, 1957
Director: Kenneth G. Crane
Category: Science Fiction/Giant Bug

THE MONSTER THAT CHALLENGED THE WORLD
Production: USA, 1957
Director: Arnold Laven
Category: Science Fiction

NOT OF THIS EARTH
Production: USA, 1957
Director: Roger Corman
Category: Science Fiction/Horror
One of Corman's best from the 50s, featuring a vampire from outer space. The stylishly evil alien has blank eyes which can burn out a human brain, so it wears wrapround shades to go with its black sharkskin suit and medical bag of blood-draining equipment. Pointlessly remade in 1988, with porn starlet Traci Lords.

PLAN 9 FROM OUTER SPACE
Production: USA, 1957
Director: Ed Wood Jr
Original title: **Grave Robbers From Outer Space**
Category: Science Fiction

QUATERMASS II
Production: UK, 1957
Director: Val Guest
US release title: **Enemy From Space**
Category: Science Fiction

A film version of Nigel Kneale's second **Quatermass** TV serial, and a follow-up to Hammer's **The Quatermass X-periment**, again featuring Brian Donlevy as the Professor, and Val Guest once more as director. In a plot strongly reminiscent of Don Siegel's **Invasion Of The Body-Snatchers**, alien forces take over humans as before, although this time much more surreptitiously as part of a plot to infiltrate an industrial research plant and use its facilities to effect an adjustment to the Earth's environment. Quatermass, by a series of investigations, learns that the aliens have infiltrated the very Government, and that the plant, Wynerton Flats, is the nerve centre of their activity. Like Siegel's film, **Quatermass II** rises from its quiet beginnings into an uncontrollable spiral of paranoia; the brilliant monochrome photography, and use of desolate, almost unearthly landscapes as analogues of a disinherited unconscious serve to compound an overall feel of terminal dread and imminent human extinction.

SHE DEVIL
Production: USA, 1957
Director: Kurt Neumann
Category: Science Fiction/Horror

A scientist develops a serum that fights disease by boosting the body's adaptive powers; when he tests it in a terminally ill woman, she not only recovers but becomes evil and twisted – a female monster whose hair colour changes with her moods. Almost indestructible, she embarks on a murder spree that sees her emerge unscathed from fatal car crashes, forcing the doctor to reverse his cure in a bid to stop her. A superb pulp SF movie by Neumann, who the following year directed his genre masterpiece, **The Fly**, and then died just weeks after its premiere.

SUPA JAIANTSU
("Super Giant")
Production: Japan, 1957
Director: Various
Category: Science Fiction

The first major *tokusatsu* film serial was Shintoho's **Supa Jaiantsu** of 1957-59 (episodes of which were later edited into four composite films for American TV, of which the best remains **Evil Brain From Outer Space**). The series ran to nine instalments: **Supa Jaiantsu** (Teruo Ishii, 1957); **Zoku Supa Jaiantsu** (Teruo Ishii, 1957); **Supa Jaiantsu kaiseijin no majo** (Teruo Ishii, 1957); **Supa Jaiantsu chikyu metsubo sunzen** (Teruo Ishii, 1957); **Supa Jaiantsu Jinko eisei to jinrui no hametsu** (Teruo Ishii, 1957); **Supa Jaiantsu uchutei to jinko eisei no gekitotsu** (Teruo Ishii, 1958); **Supa Jaiantsu uchu kaijin shutsugen** (Teruo Ishii, 1958); **Zoku Supa Jaiantsu akuma no keshin** (Chogi Akasaka, 1959); and **Zoku Supa Jaiantsu Dokuga Okoku** (Chogi Akasaka, 1959). The advent of **Supa Jaiantsu** was followed in 1958 by the television series **Gekko Kamen**; these paved the way for the definitive 60s *tokusatsu* series **Urutora Kyu** and **Urutora Shirizu**. Like **Gojira**, **Urutora Shirizu** was created by special effects master Eiji Tsuburaya, and was the first work to show a superhero growing to gigantic proportions in order to battle monsters. A notable early *tokusatsu*/SF feature film was **Uchu Kaisoku-sen** (1961, released in the USA as **Invasion Of The Neptune Men**), featuring an extremely young Shinichi "Sonny" Chiba as hero Iron Sharp, and including real WW2 firebombing footage to depict the destruction of Tokyo. Chiba also starred in **Ogon Batto** ("Golden Bat", 1966), a live-action movie depicting the adventures of Japan's first literary superhero, created in 1930 by pulp writer Ichiro Suzuki and illustrator Takeo Nagamatsu. This skull-faced protector also featured in a classic 52-part *anime* television series produced in 1967.

20 MILLION MILES TO EARTH
Production: USA, 1957
Director: Nathan Juran
Category: Science Fiction

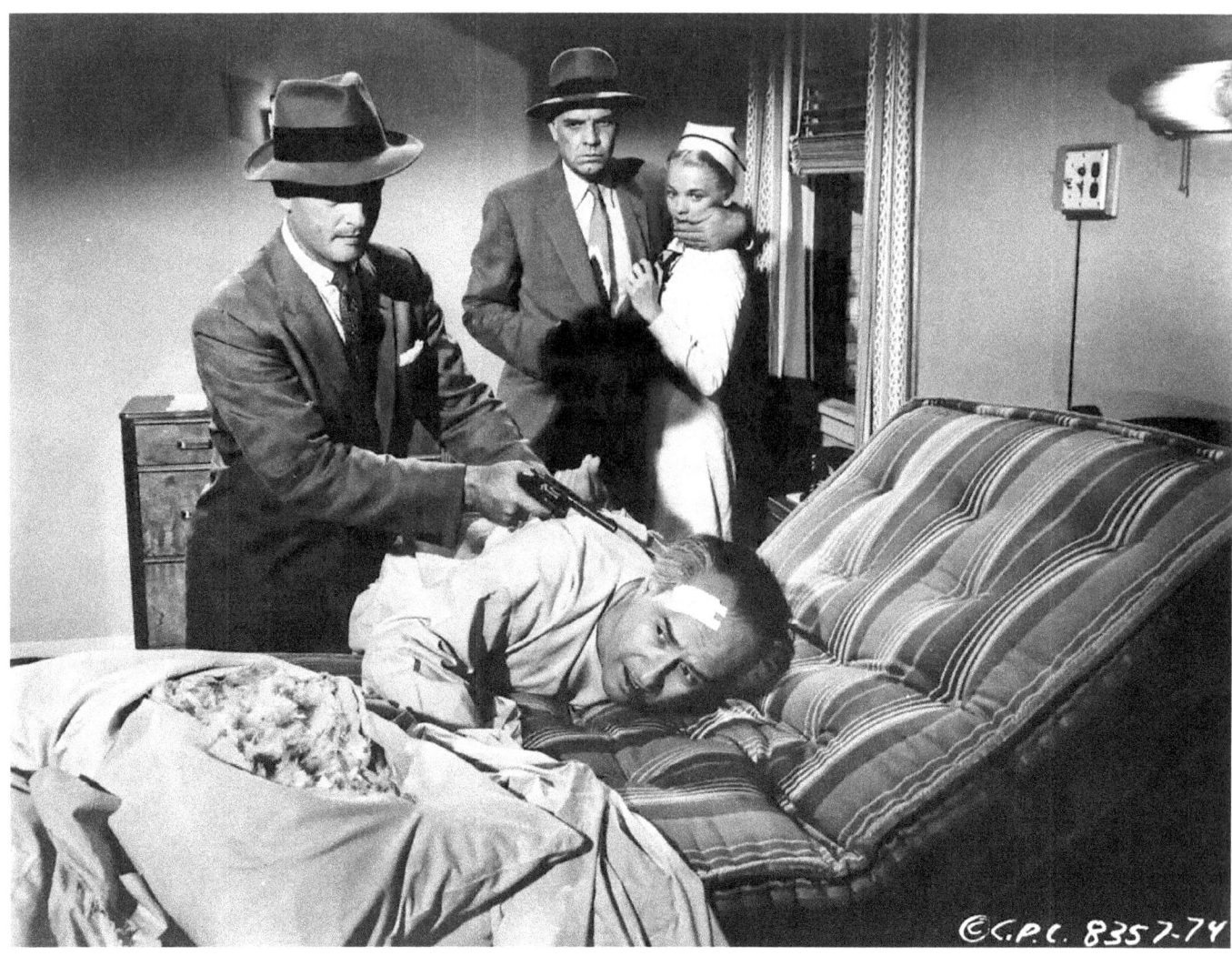

THE 27TH DAY
Production: USA, 1957
Director: William Aher
Category: Science Fiction
From John Mantley's allegorical SF novel, in which five humans in various locations on Earth are given a box of capsules by an alien. They are told that the capsules have the power to wipe out human life from entire continents, but only they can activate them. The film shows how each individual comes under intense pressure to use this weapon to annihilate his own country's enemies, until they are forced to hide away from society. Finally, it transpires that the alien was merely testing their moral resolve and maturity; as a reward for resisting temptation, the capsules now kill every evil-doer on Earth, leaving alive only those who wish for peace and freedom.

THE UNEARTHLY
Production: USA, 1957
Director: Boris Petroff
Category: Science Fiction/Horror

THE UNKNOWN TERROR
Production: USA, 1957
Director: Charles Marquis Warren
Category: Science Fiction/Horror

ATTACK OF THE 50 FOOT WOMAN
Production: USA, 1958
Director: Nathan Juran
Category: Science Fiction
An alcoholic woman (played by Allison Hayes) is turned into a giant by an alien and goes after her abusive husband. Bad special effects and only a few good moments of wanton destruction, but the avenging Hayes looks great in her bra and skirt.

ATTACK OF THE PUPPET PEOPLE
Production: USA, 1958
Director: Bert I. Gordon
Category: Science Fiction
Gordon follows up his bold **Amazing Colossal Man** by examining the other end of the scale, as an insane doll-maker reduces humans to miniature. It remains to the imagination as to whether some, like Gulliver, ended up as human dildos.

BIJO TO EKITAI NINGEN
("The Beauty And The Liquefied Man")
Production: Japan, 1958
Director: Honda Ishiro
Category: Science Fiction
A downbeat trip from Toho Studios and Honda, the king of Japanese SF cinema. In **Bijo To Ekitai Ningen**, a drug-dealer is exposed to nuclear radiation and contaminates everybody he touches, turning them to radioactive fluid. The film's title reflects the presence throughout of scantily-clad girls, while the narrative itself resonates with post-Atomic angst, the screen awash with heavy liquid visions which fuel the pulp plotline. Honda was best known for his *kaiju eiga* (monster movies), onslaughts of acid bubblegum reptilia in which prehistoric creatures like Gojira are

awoken by atomic blasts to endlessly replay the destruction of Tokyo. **Bijo To Ekitai Ningen** can be seen as a natural, more adult and pessimistic progression from Toho's earlier **Tomei Ningen** (1954), and stands among the best of the numerous "human mutant" films produced by the company, a group of works which also includes **Gasu Ningen Dai 1 Go** ("Human Gas #1", Honda, 1960), **Denso Ningen** ("Human Teleportation", Jun Fukuda, also 1960), and the later **Ido Zero Daisakusen** ("Latitude Zero: Great Operation Plan", Honda, 1969) which features human organ transplanting and animal hybrids.

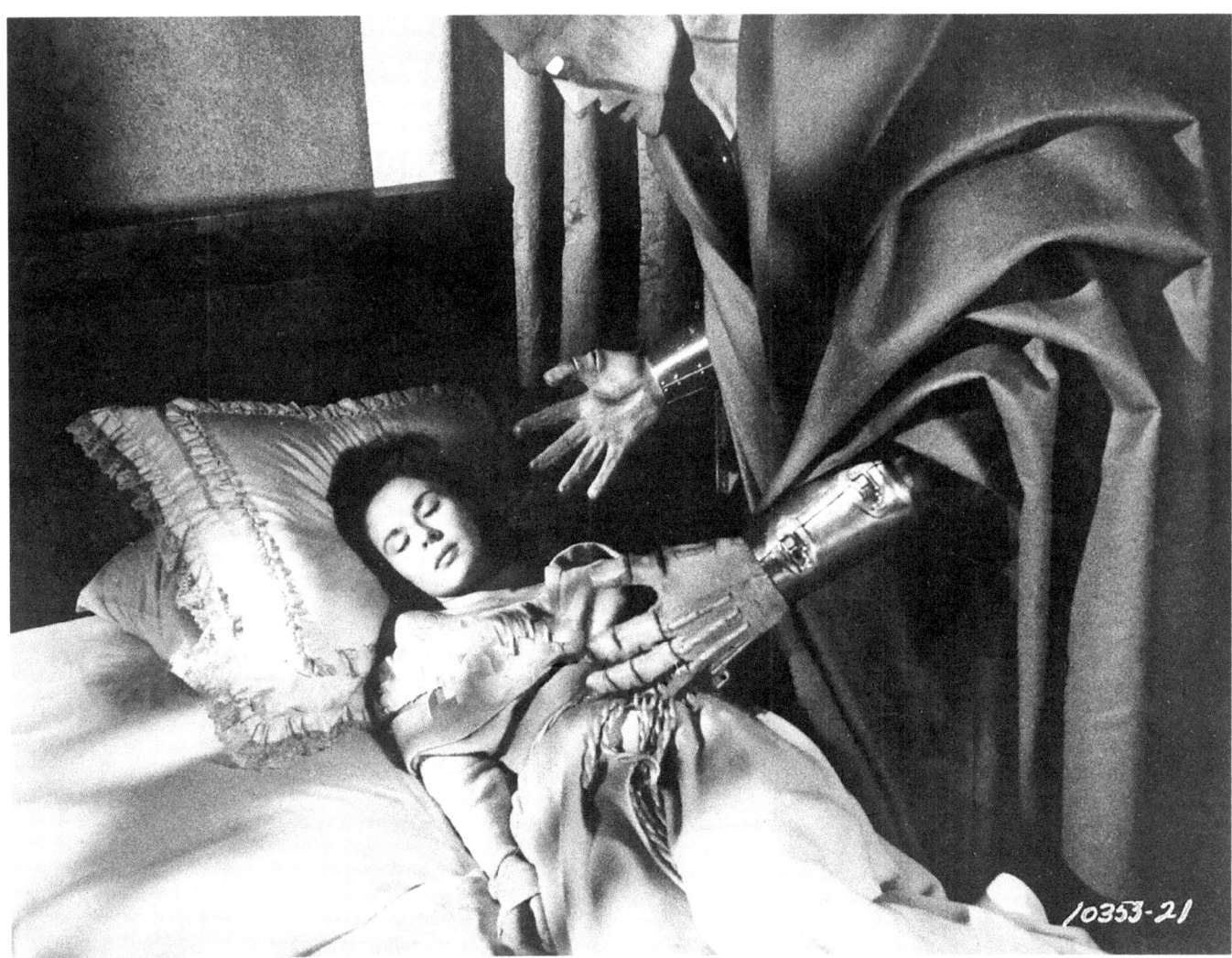

THE COLOSSUS OF NEW YORK
Production: USA, 1958
Director: Eugène Lourié
Category: Science Fiction
A menacing addition to the prevalent robot theme of the period. Essentially a set designer, Lourié's only other features for the big screen were in the "giant monster" category: **The Beast From 20,000 Fathoms, Behemoth The Sea Monster,** and **Gorgo.**

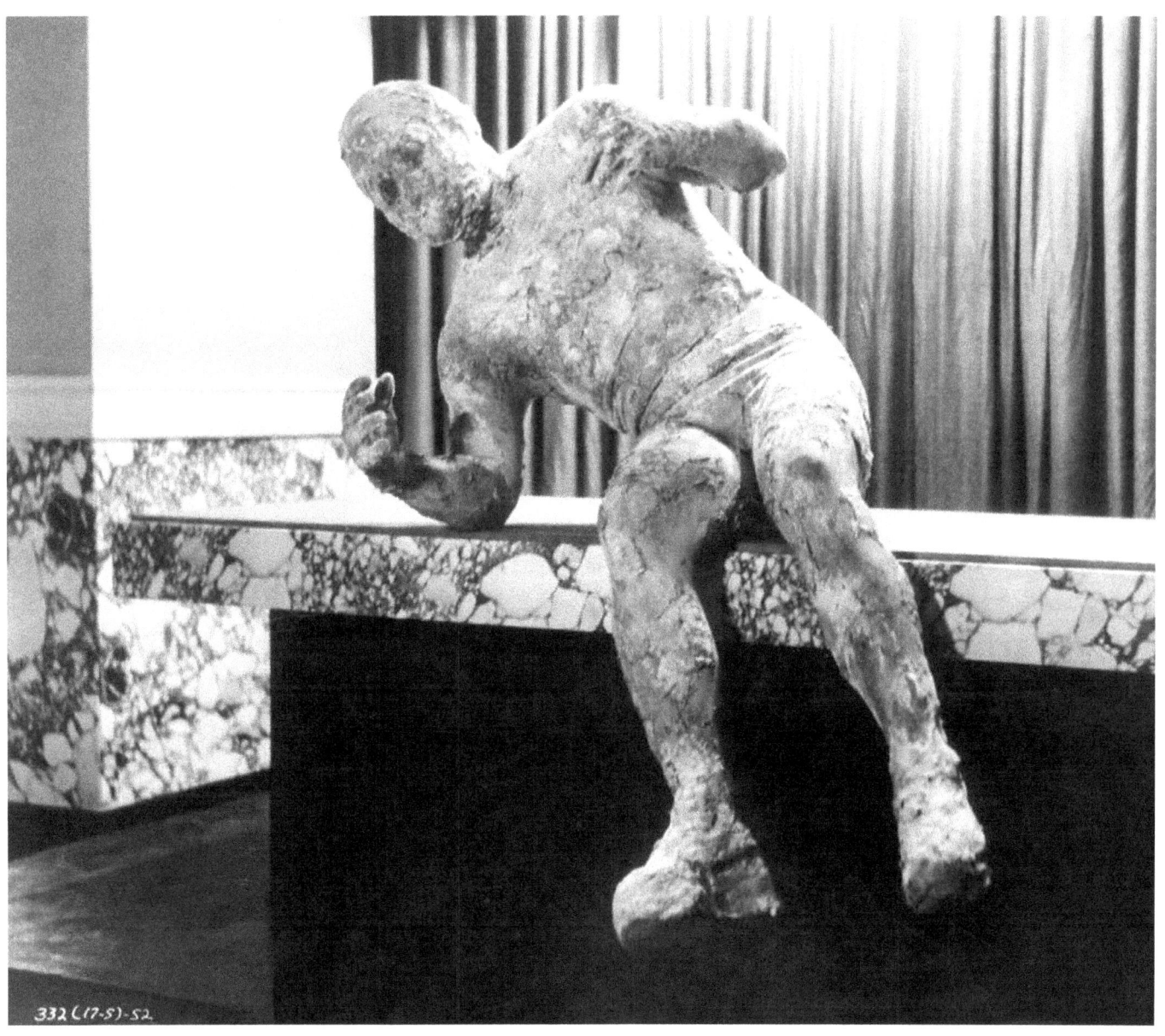

CURSE OF THE FACELESS MAN
Production: USA, 1958
Director: Edward L. Cahn
Category: Science Fiction/Horror

EARTH VS THE SPIDER
Production: USA, 1958
Director: Bert I. Gordon
Category: Science Fiction/Giant Bug

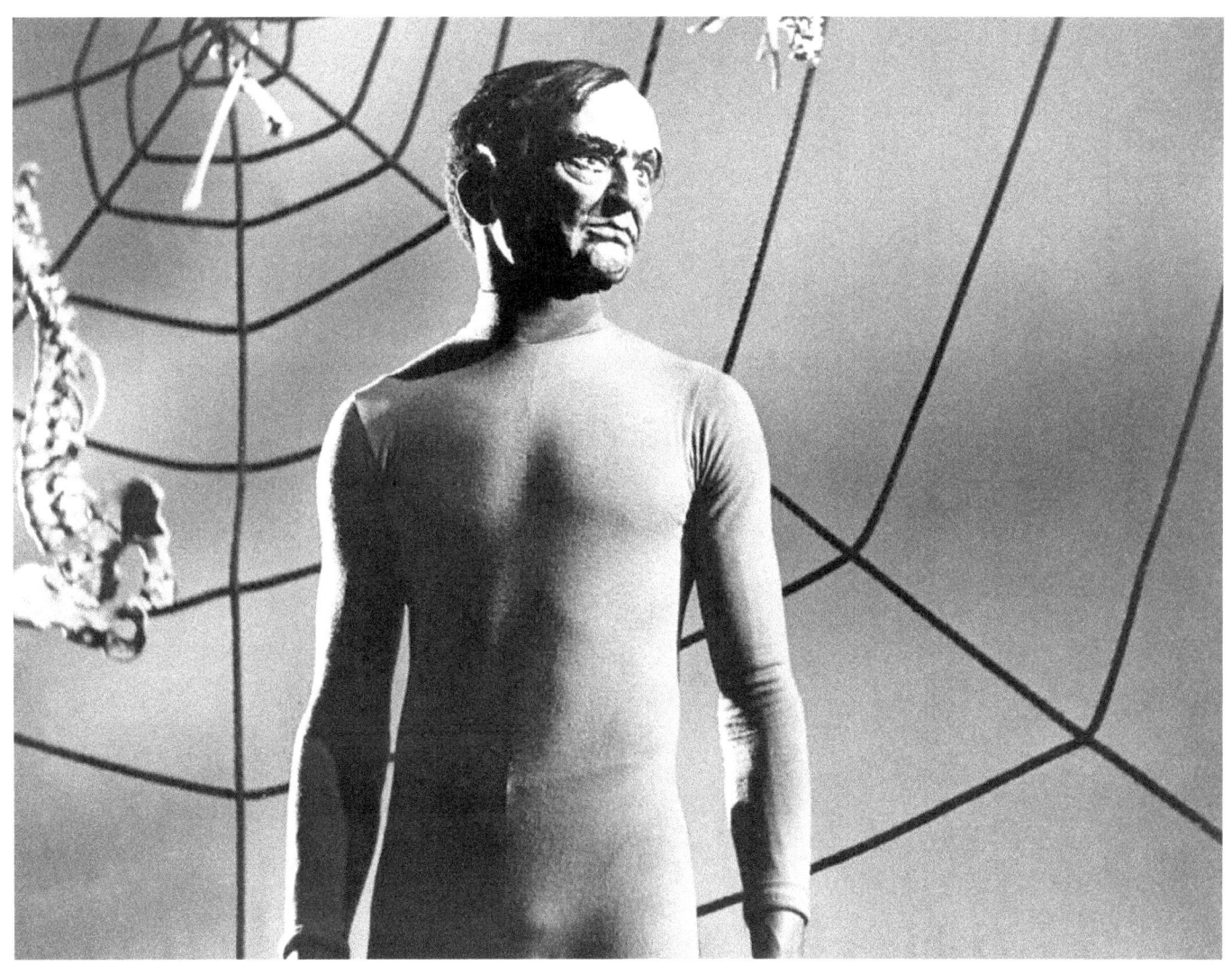

THE ELECTRONIC MONSTER
Production: UK, 1958
Director: Montgomery Tully, David Paltenghi
Category: Science Fiction

FIEND WITHOUT A FACE
Production: USA, 1958
Director: Arthur Crabtree
Category: Science Fiction/Horror
From "The Thought Monster", a 1930s pulp magazine story by Amelia Reynolds Long, this is a twisted tale of creatures made from human thought, who assume the form of a disembodied cerebellum after sucking out the brains of screaming victims.

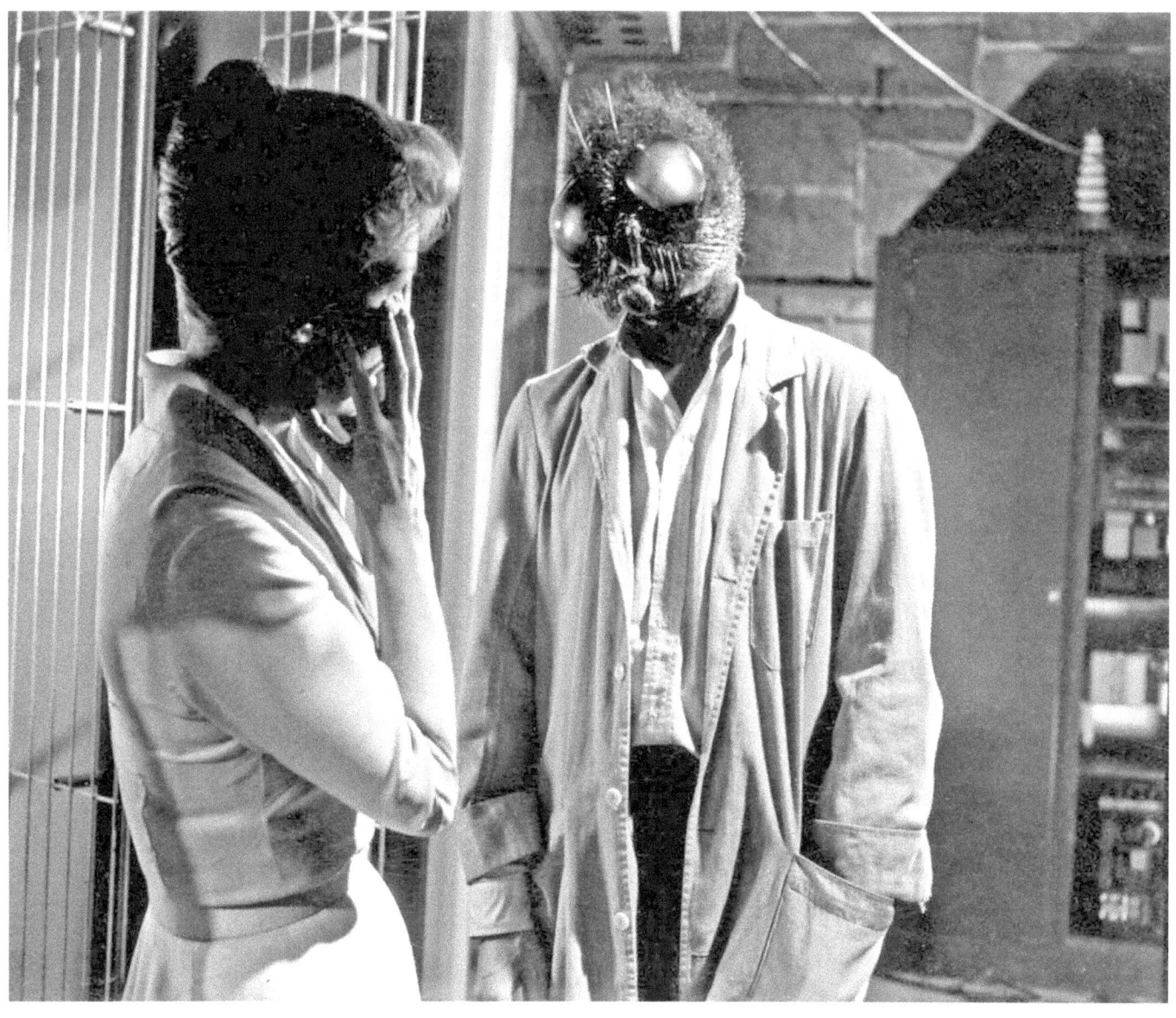

THE FLY
Production: USA, 1958
Director: Kurt Neumann
Category: Science Fiction/Horror

One of of the all-time classic SF films, in which a scientist experimenting with the teleportation of matter becomes trapped with a fly, and the atoms of the two creatures intermingle with horrifying results. The masterpiece of hybrid-horror. Price returned in a sequel, **Return Of The Fly**, a yen Of The Fly, a year later, but Don Sharp's **Curse Of The Fly**, made in 1965, was perhaps more interesting.

GIANT FROM THE UNKNOWN
Production: USA, 1958
Director: Richard E. Cunha
Category: Science Fiction/Horror

THE HIDEOUS SUN DEMON
Production: USA, 1958
Director: Robert Clarke, Tom Boutress
Category: Science Fiction/Horror

I MARRIED A MONSTER FROM OUTER SPACE
Production: USA, 1958
Director: Gene Fowler Jr
Category: Science Fiction

IT! THE TERROR FROM BEYOND SPACE
Production: USA, 1958
Director: Edward L. Cahn
Category: Science Fiction

MISSILE TO THE MOON
Production: USA, 1958
Director: Richard E. Cunha
Category: Science Fiction

MONSTER ON THE CAMPUS
Production: USA, 1958
Director: Jack Arnold
Category: Science Fiction/Horror

LA MORTE VIENE DALLO SPAZIO
("Death From Space")
Production: Italy/France, 1958
Director: Paolo Heusch
English release title: **The Day The Sky Exploded**
Category: Science Fiction
This was the first ever pure SF film shot in Italy. It also has photography and special effects by the great Mario Bava. Earth is under threat of destruction from a swarm of meteorites, and scientists must race against time to avert catastrophe.

NIGHT OF THE BLOOD BEAST
Production: USA, 1958
Director: Bernard L. Kowalski
Category: Horror

QUEEN OF OUTER SPACE
Production: USA, 1958
Director: Edward Bernds
Category: Science Fiction

Astronauts land on Venus and are surprised to find it populated by hot mini-skirted babes in low-cut tops and spiky heels; unfortunately the babes are ruled by the bitter, man-hating Queen Ilyana, who wears a mask (as do her bodyguards) to hide her disfigured face. Zsa-Zsa Gabor plays Talia, a rebel girl who loves men and leads a secret cabal who wish to usurp the evil Queen. Finally, even the Queen admits she can't live without male company, and all three factions bond in a (restrained) love-in. The film also includes scenes with a giant spider taken from the earlier **World Without End** (1956), a time-warp trip which also features space travellers and a society of sex-hungry women, this time on a mutant-infested earth of the future.

SHE DEMONS
Production: USA, 1958
Director: Richard E. Cunha
Category: Horror/Science Fiction
One of the first in the cycle of "Nazi-SF" movies that surfaced in the 50s and 60s, concerning a deranged SS war criminal on a remote island who turns a group of bikini-clad females into disfigured monsters in bamboo cages. With some exotic dancing amidst the mutilation and torture, **She Demons** is pure exploitation with an SS twist.

THE SPACE CHILDREN
Production: USA, 1958
Director: Jack Arnold
Category: Science Fiction

THE STRANGE WORLD OF PLANET X
Production: UK, 1958
Director: Gilbert Gunn
Category: Science Fiction/Giant Bug

THE TROLLENBERG TERROR
Production: UK, 1958
Director: Quentin Lawrence
US release title: **The Crawling Eye**
Category: Science Fiction

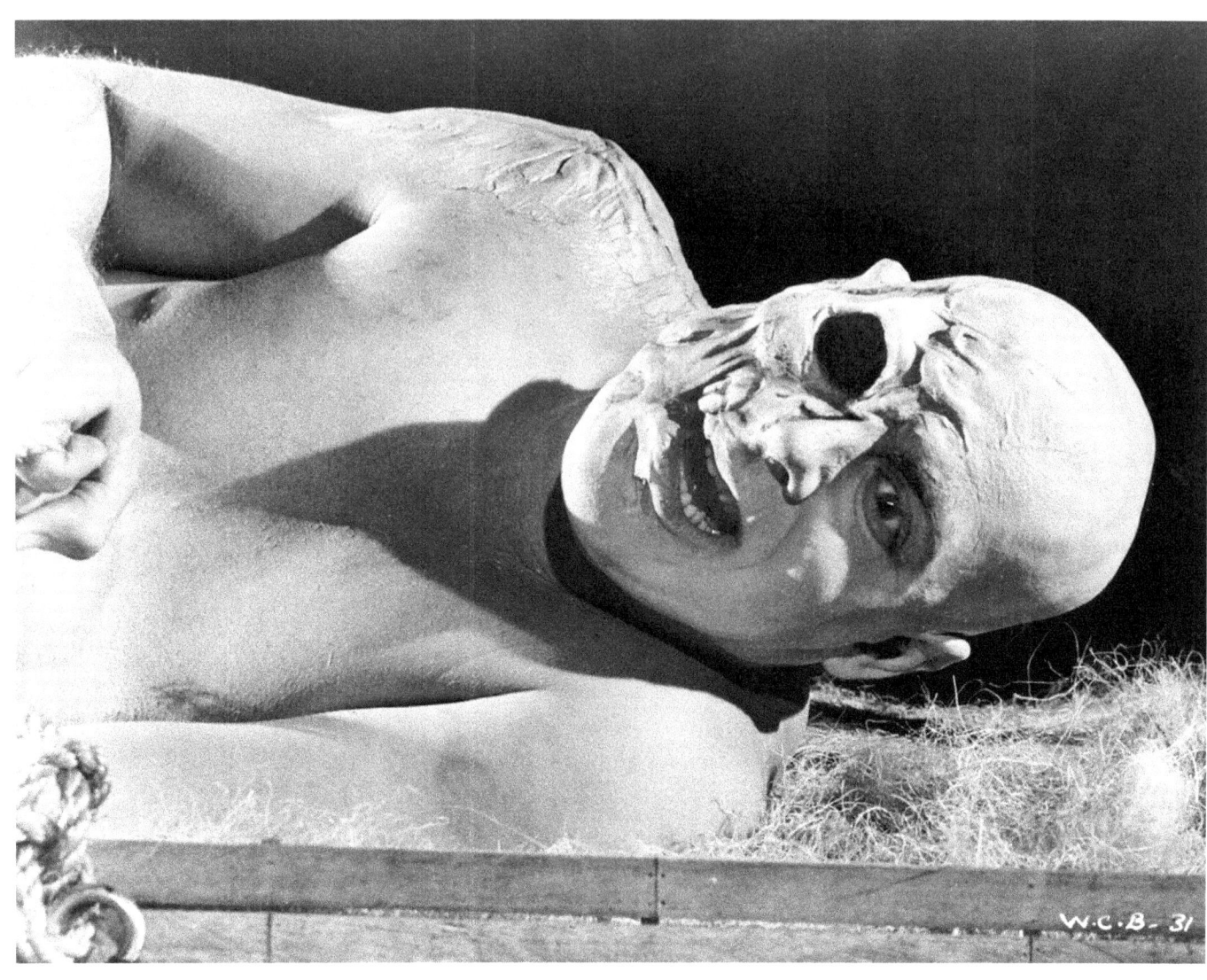

WAR OF THE COLOSSAL BEAST
Production: USA, 1958
Director: Bert I. Gordon
Category: Science Fiction

THE ALLIGATOR PEOPLE
Production: USA, 1959
Director: Roy Del Ruth
Category: Science Fiction
Scientist develops serum from alligator glands and injects it into a patient, curing his injuries but turning him into an alligator-creature with leathery skin. Nice make-up, but it might have been more piquant to use a real-life circus freak suffering from ichthyosis ("fish skin syndrome"), such as the legendary Emmet Bejano or John H Williams. Lon Chaney Jr "plays" a drunk cajun hunter whose hand was bitten off and eaten by one of the swamp reptiles.

ANGRY RED PLANET

Production: USA, 1959
Director: Ib Melchior
Category: Science Fiction

Produced by Sid Pink and distributed by AIP, this low-budget proto-psychedelic SF movie is one of the strangest in the genre. A traumatised female astronaut recounts a trip to Mars, seen in trippy flashbacks. Most alarming of the planet's creatures is a huge bat/crab/rat hybrid. Filmed in a process dubbed Cinemagic, to enhance the film's other-worldly qualities; the result was a blood-red tint with solarised highlights.

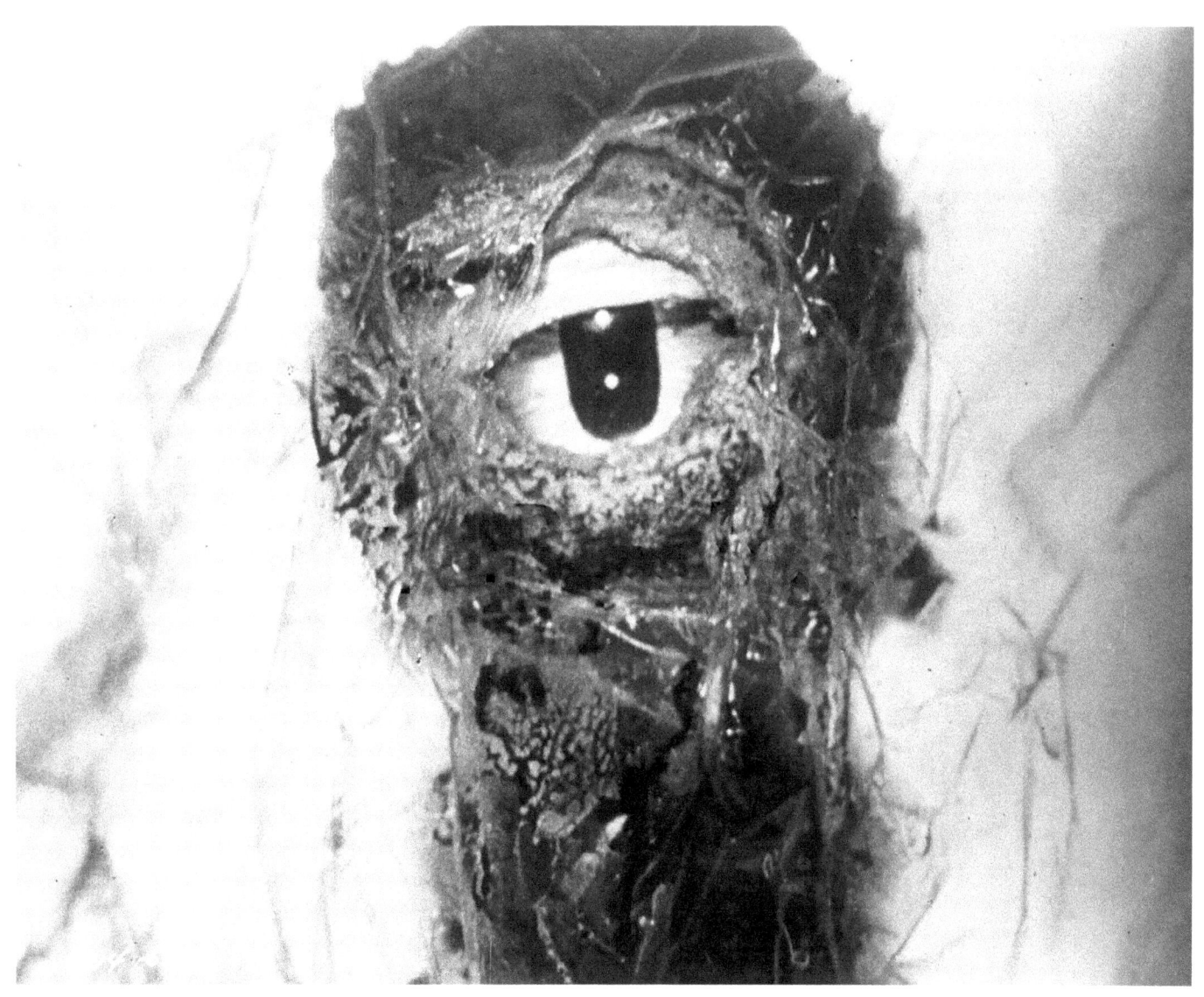

THE ATOMIC SUBMARINE
Production: USA, 1959
Director: Spemcer Gordon Bennet
Category: Science Fiction

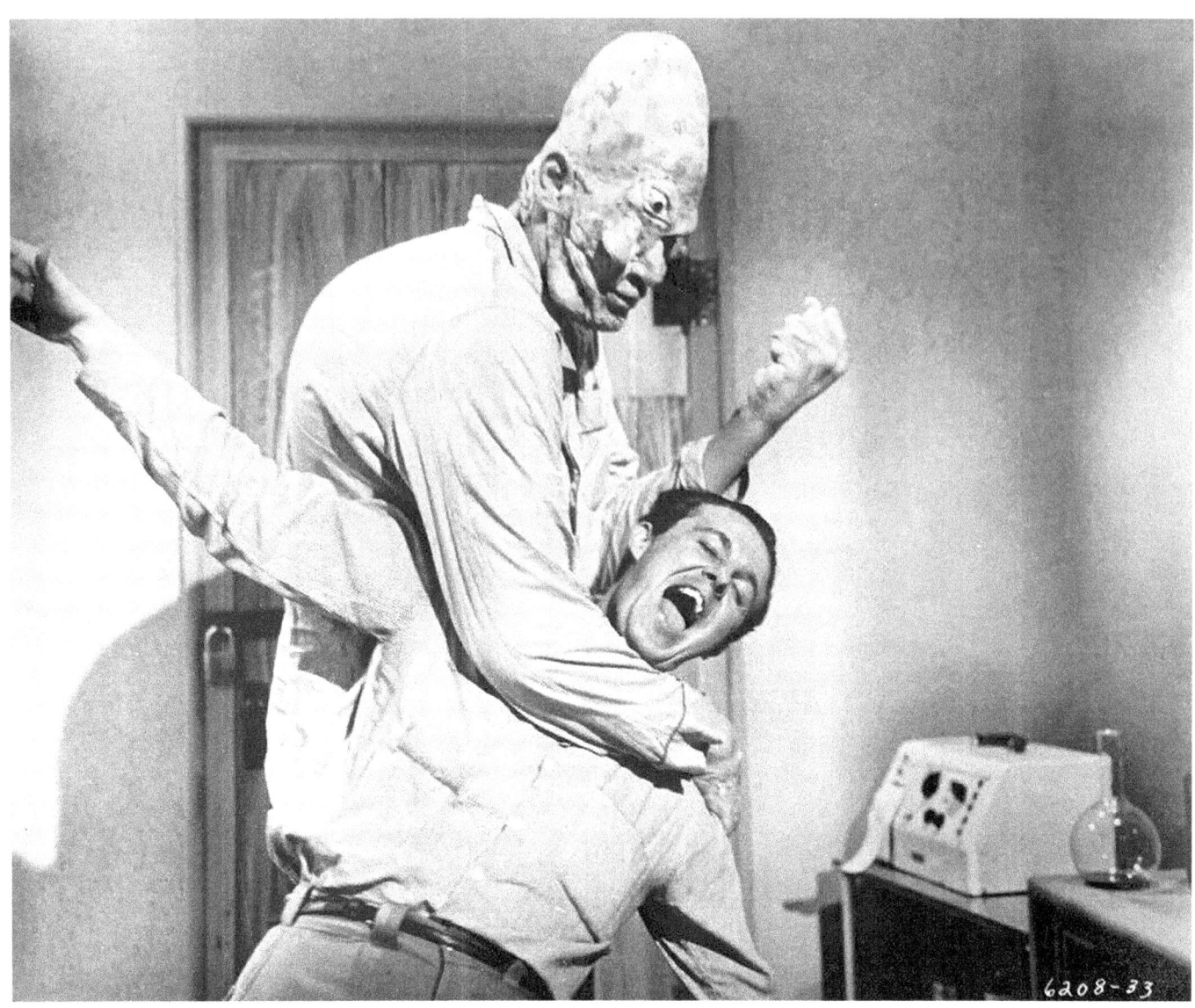

THE BRAIN THAT WOULDN'T DIE
Production: USA, 1959
Director: Joseph Green
Category: Science Fiction

Weirdest of a weird sub-genre, the living severed head movie. A crazed scientist is trying to find the perfect sexy body on which to graft his decapitated girlfriend's head, which he keeps alive in his lab. While he scours the local strip clubs, the head forges a telepathic link with a deformed mutant, the victim of previous experiments. There are elements of early sexploitation as well as horror, and the film ends with dismemberment and fiery death. A distributor by trade, Green's other main attributed directorial work was a dream sequence of psychedelic erotica which he spliced into an imported copy of the Japanese "pink" movie **Daydream**.

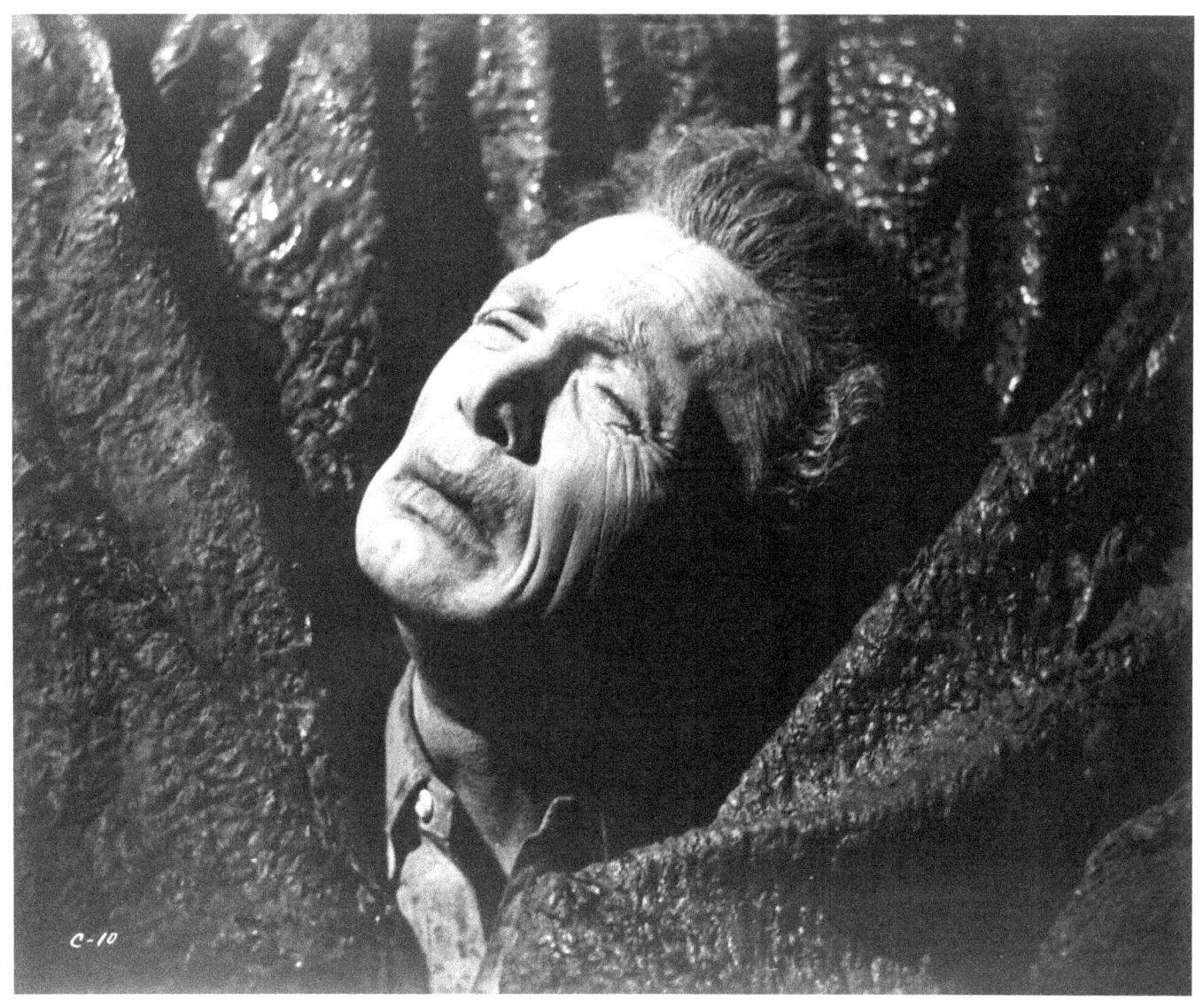

CALTIKI, IL MOSTRO IMMORTALE
("Caltiki, The Immortal Monster")
Production: Italy, 1959
Director: Riccardo Freda
Category: Science Fiction/Horror
An amorphous slime creature is discovered in Mayan ruins. Fairly dull, despite the camerawork of Mario Bava.

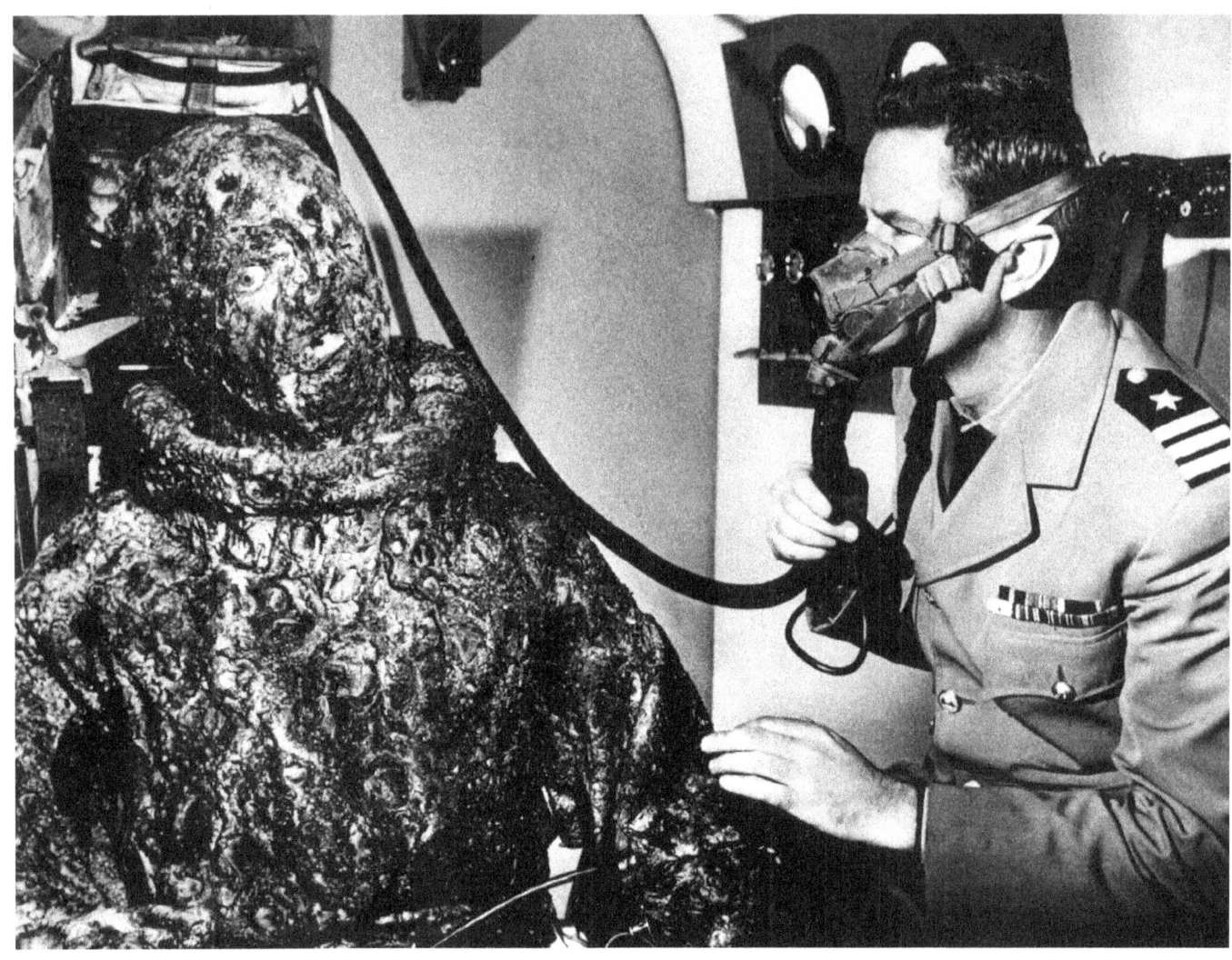

FIRST MAN INTO SPACE
Production: UK, 1959
Director: Robert Day
Category: Science Fiction/Horror

4-D MAN
Production: USA, 1959
Director: Irvin S. Yeaworth Jr.
Category: Science Fiction

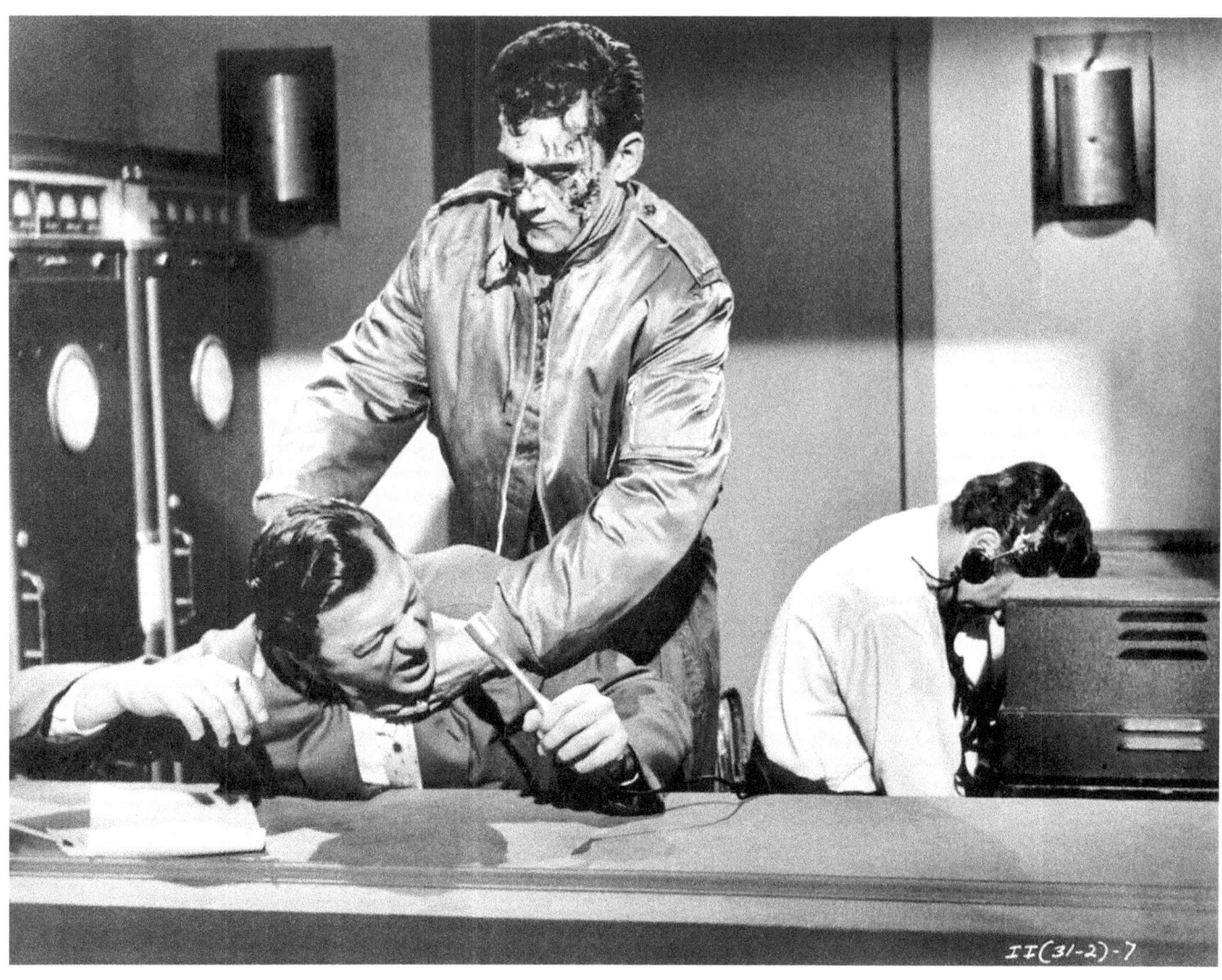

INVISIBLE INVADERS
Production: USA, 1959
Director: Edward L. Cahn
Category: Science Fiction

THE KILLER SHREWS
Production: USA, 1959
Director: Ray Kellogg
Category: Science Fiction/Horror

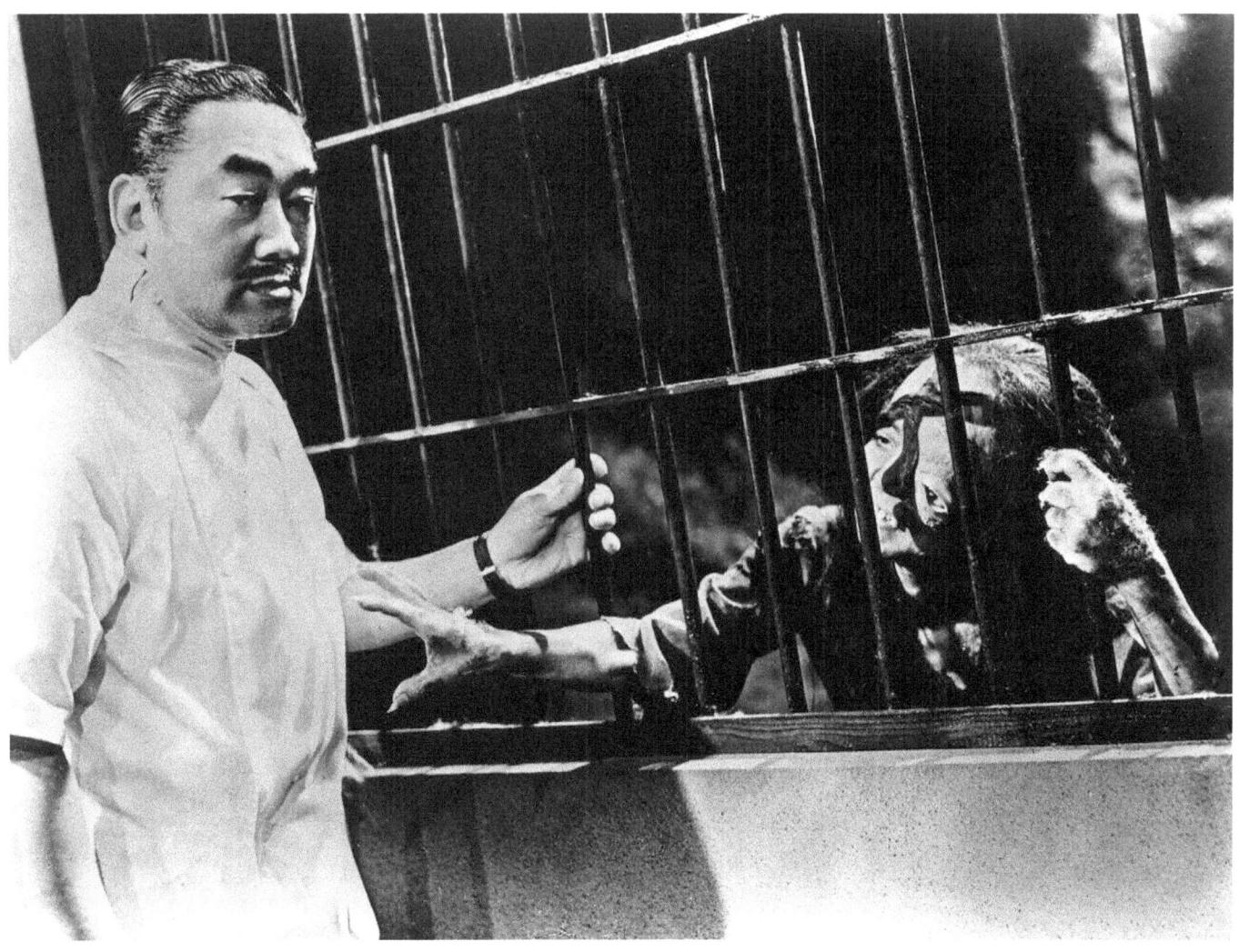

THE MANSTER
Production: Japan/USA, 1959
Director: George P. Breakston, Kenneth G. Crane
Category: Science Fiction/Horror

THE MONSTER OF PIEDRAS BLANCAS
Production: USA, 1959
Director: Irvin Berwick
Category: Science Fiction/Horror

NEBO ZOVYOT
("The Heavens Beckon")
Production: USSR, 1959
Director: Mikhail Karzhukov, Aleksandr Kozyr
US release title: **Battle Beyond The Sun**
Category: Science Fiction

Pioneering Russian SF movie featuring advanced special effects way ahead of their contemporary Western counterparts. One of several films (including **Planeta Bur**) picked up by Roger Corman for US distribution; Corman called in his young protegé, one Francis Ford Coppola, to recut the film, with added scenes, for Stateside consumption. The resultant travesty was retitled **Battle Beyond The Sun**, dragging the film back into the trash genre it had already superseded. In its original form, **Nebo Zovyot** is still the technical equal of most films produced in the subsequent decades of the 20th century.

RETURN OF THE FLY
Production: USA, 1959
Director: Edward Bernds
Category: Science Fiction

THE TWILIGHT ZONE
Production: USA, 1959-64
Director: Various
Category: Science Fiction/Fantasy/Horror
The most famous SF/fantasy show of them all, running for 151 episodes. With the script-writing mostly taken up by Richard Matheson, Charles Beaumont, and series producer/host Rod Serling – with the occasional guest writer such as Ray Bradbury (**I Sing The Body Electric**) – this was a project of sustained quality and pervasive influence. Episodes to gain legendary status include **Nightmare At 20,000 Feet**, with William Shatner, and **The Howling Man**, with John Carradine. Serling, a former WW2 combatant, also took the opportunity to pass on a "serious" message on the nature of evil in the episode **Death's-Head Revisited**, in which a gloating former Nazi torturer at Auschwitz is driven mad by the ghosts of his victims. The phrase "twilight zone" has now entered common parlance, and the show's spooky theme music by Bernard Herrmann is instantly recognizable. Serling's next series was **Night Gallery**, an occult show of variable quality that ran for 90 episodes betwen 1970 and 1972.

UCHU DAISENSO
("Great Space War")
Production: Japan, 1959
Director: Ishiro Honda
English release title: **Battle In Outer Space**
Category: Science Fiction

WASP WOMAN
Production: USA, 1959
Director: Roger Corman
Category: Science Fiction

Probably produced by Corman to cash in on the then-recent success of **The Fly**, **Wasp Woman** is a cheap, inferior effort, lacking the flashes of pulp brilliance that elevated some of Corman's other low-budget flicks of the 1950s (such as **The Undead**). More interesting is the real-life case of the film's star, Susan Cabot, who in 1986 was beaten to death with a weightlifting bar-bell by her son, a deformed dwarf. The theme of a queen wasp/human mutation was treated far more effectively in **Zzzzz** (1964, starring the stunning Joanna Frank), an episode of **The Outer Limits**.

REBEL GIRLS
Production: Philippines, 1957
Director: Unconfirmed
Category: Sexploitation

SEX

NAKED AFRICA
Production: USA, 1957
Director: Ray Phoenix
Category: Ethno-Documentary
Ethno-documentary promising "primitive passions, shocking dance of the virgins, weird ceremonies that defy belief", with the title acting a lure for those eager to scrutinize the naked bodies of young black females.

È ARRIVATA LA PARIGINA
("The Girl From Paris Is Here")
Production: Italy, 1958
Director: Camillo Mastrocinqu
Category: Sexploitation

EN CAS DE MALHEUR
("In Case Of Accident")
Production: France, 1958
Director: Claude Autant-Lara
Category: Sex/Murder

NATURISTEN-FERIEN
("Naturist Holidays")
Production: Switzerland, 1958
Director: Werner Kunz
Category: Nudism
Kunz was an advocate of the "free body" nudist movement, whose other films of naked humans cavorting include **Wir Fahren Zum Naturisten-Paradies** (1957, filmed on the Isle of Levant) and **Sonne, Meer Und Nackte Menschen** (1962, also known as **The Nude Ones**). A similar German film from 1958 was Alexander Baege's **Sensucht Nach Sonne**, known in English as **Lust For The Sun** and often wrongly attributed to Kunz.

NUDIST PARADISE
Production: USA, 1958
Director: Charles Saunders
Category: Nudism

With a prologue by the Duke of Bedford, this was the first British nudist feature film to go on general release. It had a basic plot, concerning an American who falls in love with an English naturist and joins her in a nudist camp. Other early examples of the British nudist film include Ramsay Herrington's **The Nudist Story** (1959 – "made in association with the British Sun-Bathing Association") and Arnold Miller's **Nudist Memories** (1959). Miller also made **Nudes Of The World** (1961) and **Take Off Your Clothes And Live** (1962), as well as a series of "glamour" Super-8s of the kind already being produced by George Harrison-Marks. **Travelling Light** (aka **Sunswept**, 1960), is regarded as the first genuine British naturist film, produced and directed by Edward Craven-Walker (also the inventor of the lava lamp). Walker also made **Eves On Skis** (1962). Even Michael Winner started in the nudist genre, shooting **Some Like It Cool** in 1961, whilst H. Haile Chace's **Paradisio** (1961) was perhaps the first nudie film with scenes in colour 3-D (added post-production by US distributor Jack Harris).

PRISON DES FEMMES
("Women's Prison")
Production: France, 1958
Director: Maurice Cloche
Category: Sexploitation/Prison

An early Women in Prison exploitation entry from France, which features a fair degree of topless female nudity – quite common in French cinema of the 1950s, as opposed to repressive countries such as England, where the sight of a women's naked breast was deemed "dangerous" until the late 60s. Cloche's other films included **Marchands Des Filles** (1957), a tale of white slavery set in an underworld milieu of sleaze, prostitution, crime, drugs and stripjoints, and **Les Filles De Nuit** (1958), about a murdered prostitute.

SENSUCHT NACH SONNE
("Longing For The Sun")
Production: Germany, 1958
Director: Alexander Baege
US release title: **Lust For The Sun**
Category: Nudism

TUMULTO DE PAIXÕES
("Turmoil Of Passions")
Production: Brazil/Germany/USA, 1958
Director: Zygmunt Sulistrowski
Category: Sexploitation
A film with three episodes. In the third, Celeneh Costa appears as a seductive woman, accused of witchcraft by local women and forced to return to the sea, and this became the focus of its 1962 US release entitled **The Witch Beneath The Sea**.

VOODOO VILLAGE
Altrenative title: **Sorcerer's Village**
Production: USA, 1958
Director: Hassoldt Davis
Category: Jungle Exploitation
Captain Davis and his wife, Ruth Staudinger Davis, were a latter-day couple of ethnographers who travelled across dark continents recording their findings on camera and in books. **Voodoo Village** is a visual document of their trip to the jungles of the Ivory Coast, where they went in search of the origins of African witchcraft. This culminates in a village said to be populated solely by sorcerers, who are filmed performing various bizarre rituals. Davis' first film was the short **Jungle Terror**, from

1949, and his books include *The Jungle And The Damned* which includes photographs of lepers, the mummified severed heads of prisoners executed on Devil's Island, and topless tattooed native women. The tradition of husband and wife teams in ethnographic film-making goes back to Martin and Osa Johnson, who were filming in the early 20th century; another married couple of the 1950s were William and Eve Phillips, who shot footage for a short documentary on the Indian tribes of Panama; when the film was sold on to a private production company, they decided to turn it into a work of fiction, which they did by adding stock footage and additional scenes. Key amongst these scenes were sequences filmed using half-naked Mexican hookers, hired from Tijuana bars – the result, now titled **Attack Of The Jungle Women**, was a classic example of might be termed the "ethnosploitation" genre.

ART FOR ART'S SAKE
Production: UK, 1959
Director: George Harrison Marks
Category: Glamour/Nudity
The first short glamour film made by photographer Harrison Marks and sold through the auspices of his British glamour magazine *Kamera*. The film stars nude models Pamela Green (the most famous British figure model of the 50s and 60s) and Jean Spaul, and its brief synopsis runs as follows: "Lovely Jean Spaul decides to become an artist and as her model she engages beautiful Pamela Green; anything can happen with these two together". Marks went on to produce well over 100 of these movies, until the Kamera group went bust in 1969; they featured dozens of models, and had titles like **Witches Brew**, **The French Maid**, **Night Prowler**, **Star Strip**, **Flesh And Fantasie**, **Vampire**, and **Nude Nocturne**. **Dream Goddess** (1965) was the first in colour, and by 1967/68 they started to include such "daring" features as lesbianism (eg **Garden Of Pleasure**) and SM (**Perchance To Scream**, **The Lash**, **Macabre**). In 1969 Marks started a new company, Maximus, continuing to produce 8mm sex movies for home exhibition, and often making hardcore versions of these for export. Marks had also moved into nudie feature production in 1961, directing **Naked As Nature Intended**, followed by **The Naked World of Harrison Marks** (1965) and **Nine Ages Of Nakedness** (1969).

EUROPA DI NOTTE
("Europe By Night")
Production: Italy, 1959
Director: Alessandro Blasetti
Category: Sexy Mondo
One of the first Italian proto-mondo films to deal with European culture, with the emphasis on sex (previous proto-mondo films – commencing with Gian Gaspare Napolitano's **Magia Verde** in 1952 – were all about Asian or African ethnographics). Other early films in a similar vein were Luigi Vanzi's **Il Mondo di Notte** (1959) and Gianni Proia's **Il Mondo di Notte 2** (1960), Renzo Russo's **Tropico di Notte** (1961) and **Mondo Caldo di Notte** (1962), Alessandro Jacovoni's **Universo di Notte** (1962), and Roberto Bianchi Montero's **Notti Calde d'Oriente** (1962). Films of this type would become known as "sexy nocturnes".

EN FREMMED BANKER PÅ
("A Stranger Knocks")
Production: Denmark, 1959
Director: Johan Jacobsen
US release title: **A Stranger Knocks**
Category: Sexploitation
When imported and screened in the US, this film became the subject of a landmark censorship case, inspired by scenes showing implied copulation.

THE IMMORAL MR. TEAS
Production: USA, 1959
Director: Russ Meyer
Category: Nudie-Cutie
Noteworthy as the first nudie from Meyer, who went on to become one of the biggest ditectors in sexploitation. Meyer's obsession with over-sized female breasts soon became his trade-mark, epitomised first by his own wife, Eve, and then a succession of buxotic actresses such as Lorna Maitland, Tura Satana, Uschi Digard, and many more.

KYUJU-KYUHONME NO KIMUSUME
("The 99th Virgin")
Production: Japan, 1959
Director: Magatani Morihei
English title: **Blood Sword Of The 99th Virgin**
Category: Sexploitation/Sadism
A key film in the development of Japanese exploitation cinema, the story of a mountain town whose residents worship bizarre gods, and kidnap passing virgins

for torture, crucifixion and sacrifice by holy sword. When the daughter of a local official is abducted and lined up to become the ninety-ninth victim of the blood cult, her father launches a daring rescue operation. With its then-shocking scenes of torture and scantily-clad girls, **Kyuju-Kyuhonme No Kimusume** sowed the bad seeds of a cinema where sex, cruelty and violence would collide with revolutionary impact in the mid-1960s. From Shintoho.

THE MATING URGE
Director: Howard C. Brown
Production: USA, 1959
Category: Sexology
An anthropological sexology film which purports to examine the mating rituals of various cultures, including footage filmed in Africa, South-East Asia, and Papua New Guinea. While some of the sequences seem genuine, others have no doubt been recreated for the camera. Among the subjects featured are a fertility tree, lesbian marriage with male slavery, and vine-jumping. A prime example of the zone where documentary crosses into covert sexual titillation.

NIGHT TIME
Production: USA, c.1959
Producer: Starlight Films
Category: Striptease
A prime example of the amusement arcade nudie-loops produced by Starlight and other companies during the 50s and 60s, **Night Time** stars popular model/stripper Derri Oakes. Her other films, which number in the dozens, include **Dainty Doll**, **Nude Capades**, and **Wildcat**; she was only one out of hundreds of girls who bared their

naked bodies for this uncharted cinematic sub-genre. Though relatively innocent in content, arcade loops would increase in explicitness throughout the 60s, in line with the drive-in movie. The rise of peepshow sex loops was really kick-started in 1967 when Martin Hodas – known as the "King of the Peeps" – installed his first set of coin-operated film machines in adult bookstores in New York. Relocating the machines from arcades to stores was a masterstroke which enabled Hodas to amass a fortune in very quick time; by 1970 he had progressed to private booths and was producing his own 8mm loops, which soon became hardcore in content. It was entrepreneur Reuben Sturman who eventually established a nationwide network of private sex-film booths; both men were dogged by accusations of tax evasion and having links to organised crime.

TEENAGE BRIDE
Production: USA, 1959/63
Director: Ron Ormond
Original title: **Please Don't Touch Me**
Category: Sex Exploitation

VIRGIN SACRIFICE
Production: USA, 1959
Director: Fernando Wagner
Category: Sexploitation

INDEX OF MAIN TITLES

THE ABOMINABLE SNOWMAN (1957)	90
THE ALLIGATOR PEOPLE (1959)	147
THE AMAZING COLOSSAL MAN (1957)	104, 104-5
ANGRY RED PLANET (1959)	148
ART FOR ART'S SAKE (1959)	171
ASCENSEUR POUR L'ECHAFAUD (1958)	63
THE ASTOUNDING SHE MONSTER (1957)	105
EL ATAÚD DEL VAMPIRO (1958)	23
THE ATOMIC SUBMARINE (1959)	149
ATTACK OF THE CRAB MONSTERS (1957)	106
ATTACK OF THE 50 FOOT WOMAN (1958)	124, 125
ATTACK OF THE PUPPET PEOPLE (1958)	126
BACK FROM THE DEAD (1957)	8
THE BEAT GENERATION (1959)	76, 77
BEAT GIRL (1959)	77
THE BIG OPERATOR (1959)	78
BIJO TO EKITAI NINGEN (1958)	126-128, 127
THE BLACK SCORPION (1957)	107
BLOOD OF DRACULA (1957)	9
BLOOD OF THE VAMPIRE (1958)	24
THE BLOODY BROOD (1959)	79
THE BONNIE PARKER STORY (1958)	64
THE BRAIN THAT WOULDN'T DIE (1959)	150
THE BRIDE AND THE BEAST (1958)	93
BYAKUYA NO YOJO (1958)	24
CALTIKI, IL MOSTRO IMMORTALE (1959)	151
THE CAMP ON BLOOD ISLAND (1958)	65
CAT GIRL (1957)	10
CHIKYU BOEIGUN (1957)	107, 107-108
THE COLOSSUS OF NEW YORK (1958)	128
COMPULSION (1959)	79-80
THE COOL AND THE CRAZY (1958)	66
COP HATER (1958)	67
CORRIDORS OF BLOOD (1958)	25
COVER GIRL KILLER (1959)	80
THE CRY BABY KILLER (1958)	68
THE CURSE OF FRANKENSTEIN (1957)	10, 11
CURSE OF THE FACELESS MAN (1958)	129
CURSE OF THE UNDEAD (1959)	39
DAUGHTER OF DR. JEKYLL (1957)	12
THE DEADLY MANTIS (1957)	108, 108-109
DEATH IN SMALL DOSES (1957)	56
THE DEVIL'S HAND (1959/61)	40
THE DEVIL'S PARTNER (1958)	26
DE DØDES TJERN (1958)	26
DRACULA (1958)	27
È ARRIVATA LA PARIGINA (1958)	164, 165
EARTH VS THE SPIDER (1958)	130
THE ELECTRONIC MONSTER (1958)	131
EN CAS DE MALHEUR (1958)	166
ERCOLE E LA REGINA DI LIDIA (1956)	98, 99
EUROPA DI NOTTE (1959)	171

THE FACE IN THE TOMBSTONE MIRROR (1958)	28
LE FATICHE DI ERCOLE (1958)	94, 95
FIEND WITHOUT A FACE (1958)	132
FIRST MAN INTO SPACE (1959)	152
THE FLESH AND THE FIENDS (1959)	41
THE FLY (1958)	133
4-D MAN (1959)	153
THE FOUR SKULLS OF JONATHAN DRAKE (1959)	42
FRANKENSTEIN 1970 (1958)	4, 29
FRANKENSTEIN'S DAUGHTER (1958)	30
EN FREMMED BANKER PÅ (1959)	172
FROM HELL IT CAME (1957)	109
DER FROSCHE MIT DER MASKE (1959)	80
GIANT FROM THE UNKNOWN (1958)	134
THE GIRL IN BLACK STOCKINGS (1957)	54, 55
GIRLS ON THE LOOSE (1958)	69
THE GLASS EYE (1957)	12
GRIP OF THE STRANGLER (1958)	31
EL GRITO DE LA MUERTE (1959)	42
GUNS DON'T ARGUE (1957)	57
GUNS GIRLS AND GANGSTERS (1959)	81
DIE HALBSTARKEN (1957)	58
HELL ON DEVIL'S ISLAND (1957)	59
THE HIDEOUS SUN DEMON (1958)	134, 135
HIGH SCHOOL CONFIDENTIAL (1958)	70
EL HOMBRE Y IL EL MONSTRUO (1959)	43
THE HORRORS OF THE BLACK MUSEUM (1959)	82
HOT ROD RUMBLE (1957)	60
THE HOUSE ON HAUNTED HILL (1959)	43
HOW TO MAKE A MONSTER (1958)	32
I MARRIED A MONSTER FROM OUTER SPACE (1958)	136
I WAS A TEENAGE FRANKENSTEIN (1957)	13
I WAS A TEENAGE WEREWOLF (1957)	7, 7
THE IMMORAL MR. TEAS (1959)	2, 173
THE INCREDIBLE SHRINKING MAN (1957)	110
INVASION OF THE SAUCER MEN (1957)	111
THE INVISIBLE BOY (1957)	102, 103
INVISIBLE INVADERS (1959)	154
IT! THE TERROR FROM BEYOND SPACE (1958)	137
JACK THE RIPPER (1959)	83
EL JINETE SIN CABEZA (1957)	91
JOOBACHI (1958-61)	71
JUNGFRUKÄLLAN (1959)	99
JUVENILE JUNGLE (1958)	72
KAIDAN KASANE-GA-FUCHI (1957)	14
THE KILLER SHREWS (1959)	155
KRONOS (1957)	112
KUMONOSU-JO (1957)	92
KYUJU-KYUHONME NO KIMUSUME (1959)	173-174, 174
LADRÓN DE CADÁVERES (1957)	14
THE LAND UNKNOWN (1957)	88, 89
MACABRE (1958)	33
MACHINE-GUN KELLY (1958)	72-73, 73
THE MAN WHO COULD CHEAT DEATH (1959)	44
THE MAN WHO TURNED TO STONE (1957)	113
THE MAN WITHOUT A BODY (1957)	114
THE MANSTER (1959)	156
THE MATING URGE (1959)	175
MISSILE TO THE MOON (1958)	138
MISTERIOS DE LA MAGIA NERA (1958)	34
MISTERIOS DE ULTRATOMBA (1959)	44
LA MOMIA AZTECA (1957)	15
THE MONOLITH MONSTERS (1957)	115
THE MONSTER FROM GREEN HELL (1957)	116
THE MONSTER OF PIEDRAS BLANCAS (1959)	157
MONSTER ON THE CAMPUS (1958)	139
THE MONSTER THAT CHALLENGED THE WORLD (1957)	117
LA MORTE VIENE DALLO SPAZIO (1958)	139
MOTORCYCLE GANG (1957)	61

Title	Page
LA MUJER Y LA BESTIA (1959)	83
THE MUMMY (1959)	45
NACHTS, WENN DER TEUFEL KAM (1957)	61-62
DIE NACKTE UND DER SATAN (1959)	46
NAKED AFRICA (1957)	164
NATURISTEN-FERIEN (1958)	166
NAZARÍN (1959)	84
NEBO ZOVYOT (1959)	157
NIGHT OF THE BLOOD BEAST (1958)	140
NIGHT OF THE DEMON (1957)	16
NIGHT TIME (c.1959)	175-176
NOT OF THIS EARTH (1957)	117
NUDIST PARADISE (1958)	167
ONNA KYUKETSUKI (1959)	47
PEEPING TOM (1959)	84-85, 85
PLAN 9 FROM OUTER SPACE (1957)	118
PRISON DES FEMMES (1958)	168
THE PURPLE GANG (1959)	86
QUATERMASS II (1957)	119
QUEEN OF OUTER SPACE (1958)	141
REBEL GIRLS (1957)	162, 163
RETURN OF DRACULA (1958)	34, 35
RETURN OF THE FLY (1959)	1, 158, 159
THE REVENGE OF FRANKENSTEIN (1958)	36
SAFETY OR SLAUGHTER (1958)	73
SAMPO (1959)	100
THE SCREAMING SKULL (1958)	37
SENSUCHT NACH SONNE (1958)	169
THE SEVENTH VOYAGE OF SINBAD (1958)	95, 95-96
SHE DEMONS (1958)	142
SHE DEVIL (1957)	119
SIGNAL 30 (1959)	86
THE SPACE CHILDREN (1958)	143
THE STRANGE WORLD OF PLANET X (1958)	144
SPOOK CHASERS (1957)	17
THE STRANGLERS OF BOMBAY (1959)	101
SUPA JAIANTSU (1957)	120, 120-121
TEENAGE BRIDE (1959)	176
TEENAGE DOLL (1957)	62-63, 62
TEENAGE MONSTER (1957)	18
TERROR IN A TEXAS TOWN (1958)	96
TERROR IS A MAN (1959)	48
VIRGIN SACRIFICE (1959)	177
THE THING THAT COULDN'T DIE (1958)	38
THE TINGLER (1959)	48-49, 49
TOKAIDO YOTSUYA KAIDAN (1959)	3, 51, 52
TOUCH OF EVIL (1958)	74
LES TRIPES AU SOLEIL (1959)	87
THE TROLLENBERG TERROR (1958)	145
TUMULTO DE PAIXÕES (1958)	170
20 MILLION MILES TO EARTH (1957)	121
THE 27TH DAY (1957)	122
THE TWILIGHT ZONE (1959-64)	159
UCHU DAISENSO (1959)	160
THE UNEARTHLY (1957)	121
THE UNKNOWN TERROR (1957)	124
THE UNEARTHLY (1957)	123
THE VAMPIRE (1957)	18, 19
I VAMPIRI (1957)	20
EL VAMPIRO (1957)	21
VERTIGO (1958)	74, 75
VIRGIN SACRIFICE (1959)	177
VOODOO ISLAND (1957)	22
VOODOO VILLAGE (1958)	170-172
WAR OF THE COLOSSAL BEAST (1958)	146
WASP WOMAN (1959)	161
THE WILD WOMEN OF WONGO (1958)	97
LES YEUX SANS VISAGE (1959)	51-52, 51, 53
YOJASO NO MAOU (1957)	22

ORGY PLUS MASSACRE
SEXY, SCARY & SENSATIONAL CINEMA 1950-1979

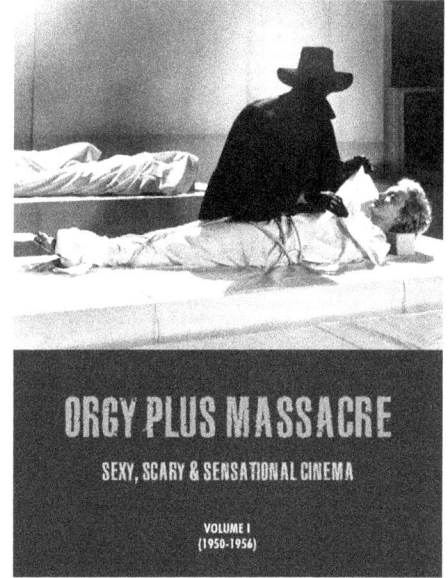

ORGY PLUS MASSACRE
SEXY, SCARY & SENSATIONAL CINEMA
VOLUME 1
(1950-1956)

ORGY PLUS MASSACRE
SEXY, SCARY & SENSATIONAL CINEMA
VOLUME 2
(1957-1959)

ORGY PLUS MASSACRE
SEXY, SCARY & SENSATIONAL CINEMA
VOLUME 3
(1960-1962)

ORGY PLUS MASSACRE
SEXY, SCARY & SENSATIONAL CINEMA
VOLUME 4
(1963-1964)

ORGY PLUS MASSACRE
SEXY, SCARY & SENSATIONAL CINEMA
VOLUME 5
(1965-1966)

SHADOWS IN A PHANTOM EYE

ATTRACTIONS & ABERRATIONS IN THE MOVING IMAGE 1872-1949

THE COMPLETE 15-VOLUME SERIES

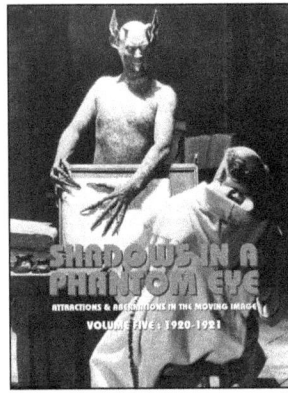   

  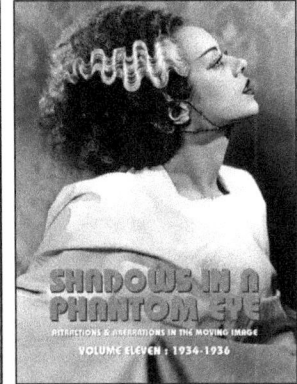 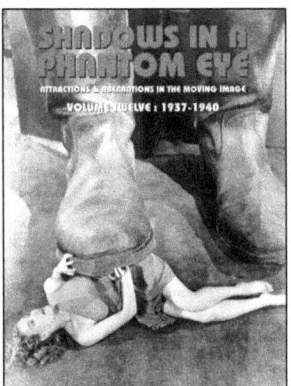

www.ingramcontent.com/pod-product-compliance
Lightning Source LLC
Chambersburg PA
CBHW061125070526
44584CB00033B/4219